BYZANTIUM
ITS TRIUMPHS AND TRAGEDY

RENÉ GUERDAN

Translated by D. L. B. Hartley

*With a Preface
by Charles Diehl*

G. P. PUTNAM'S SONS
NEW YORK

© 1957 by René Guerdan

FIRST AMERICAN EDITION

All rights reserved. This book, or parts thereof, must not be reproduced in any form without permission.

Library of Congress Catalogue
Card Number: 56-10230

MANUFACTURED IN THE UNITED STATES OF AMERICA

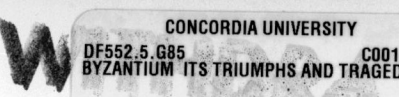

BYZANTIUM
ITS TRIUMPHS AND TRAGEDY

PLATE 1. *The Pantocratur depicted in the apse of Monreale Cathedral*

PREFACE

THE work which I have the pleasure of introducing is not merely a popularization. Certainly the personality of the Emperor Nicephorus Phocas, his campaigns and his government are fairly well known; Gustave Schlumberger's important work offers a picture of this glorious regime with perhaps, indeed, an excess of detail. But this large volume was intended for specialists and will hardly attract the general reader.

M. Guerdan has given a brief survey of the history of Byzantium and of one of her great emperors of the tenth century. But that forms only the ground plan of the book. Each event during the reign of Nicephorus was linked with accepted ideas and institutions which dominated the entire history of Byzantium. It is these ideas and institutions which M. Guerdan has described and explained; and in this undoubtedly lies the great interest of his book. In a long and excellent chapter, for example, he has explained the position of the Byzantine Emperor, the principles upon which the institution of Byzantine monarchy rested and the consequences which followed. As he has brought in many details sometimes neglected by specialists and offered many new ideas, his work will interest both the specialist and the general reader.

M. Guerdan has followed up his account of the campaigns of Nicephorus with descriptions of Byzantine military organization and the methods of Imperial diplomacy. And finally he has given a great deal of attention to those factors which perhaps determined the course of the internal history of Byzantium: the economic and social factors. All these chapters are most carefully written, but the style is lively. Few technical terms are used. This book will satisfy and interest the specialist; it will also please the general reader, for he will find in it a vivid description of Byzantine life and of the impact of the Eastern Empire upon the rest of the world.

CHARLES DIEHL

FOREWORD

IT must be admitted that in spite of several works of scholarship the history of Byzantium is very little known; the subject is perhaps even disdained.

This may be due to the unconscious survival of the hatred which existed between the Latin and Greek worlds in the Middle Ages. That hatred was once responsible for the fall of Byzantium; will it also result in the Empire being forgotten?

This double death would be a great injustice. The Eastern Empire played an impressive part in history. For ten centuries it was the ever-ready, ever-besieged, ever-resisting rampart of Christianity against the steadily mounting waves of barbarism—a tide as powerful as that of the Germans, comprising as it did the Slavs, Bulgars and above all Moslems. The Crusades of which we are so proud cannot compare with the prodigious struggle, marked by resounding triumphs and unexpected reverses, which the Byzantines maintained against all the forces of Islam from the time of Heraclius to the death of Constantine Dragases.

What Empire ever did more for civilization? First, it preserved civilization. While the West was slumbering through the night of the early Middle Ages, bereft of learning, of organized civil life and tradition, Byzantium remained the sole repository of the glories of Greece and Rome. But civilization was not only preserved; through her efforts it grew and spread. Her monks and missionaries travelled widely, and led more than half of Europe out of savagery and paganism. Under Justinian they made contact with the Huns of Moesia, the Goths of the Crimea, the Abasgians of the Caucasus and they reached the much more distant people of Ethiopia, Ceylon, the Malabar Coast and China, from which country they brought back the silk worm, as yet unknown in Europe; under Heraclius they influenced the Croatians and Serbs and under the reign of Michael III the Bulgars, Moravians, Khazars and Russians; under Basil I the Narentians, under Constantine VII the Hungarians, and the Petchenegs during the reign of Constantine Monomachus.

Finally, we ourselves owe everything to the Eastern Empire, for the Renaissance, which has made us what we are, would not have taken place without it. François Lenormant has written: 'If the importance of the fugitives of 1453 has been exaggerated, for its impact was but a second-rate one, the arrival in Florence of the great Byzantine scholars—of Bessarion, Gennadios, Gemistus Plethon, of Mark of Ephesus—as representatives of the Greek church on the Council, the resulting relationship which matured between them and the Italian scholars brought true enlightenment to Italy. It was then that Ancient Greece was revealed to the West; it is from that moment that one must date the literary Renaissance.'

This book is offered as something more than a popularization. It is a tribute to a civilization which, although far from perfect, does not deserve to be left in oblivion.

RENÉ GUERDAN

CONTENTS

PREFACE BY CHARLES DIEHL　　　　　　　　page 5
FOREWORD　　　　　　　　　　　　　　　　　7

I   THE KINGDOM OF CHRIST ON EARTH
    Christ Incarnate　　　　　　　　　　　　　17
    A State with the Gospel for Constitution　　　29
    Other Religious Groups within the Empire　　39
    The Angels　　　　　　　　　　　　　　　45
    Party Politics　　　　　　　　　　　　　　48
    The Hippodrome—an Ersatz Forum　　　　53
    The Empire of Miracles and Palmistry　　　64
    Appendix. The Bogomile Heresy　　　　　74

II SOCIAL STRIFE AND ECONOMIC STABILITY
    A Strange Class War　　　　　　　　　　81
    A Paradise of Privilege and Monopoly　　　86

III THE BASILEUS GOES TO WAR
    The Army　　　　　　　　　　　　　　　107
    A Basileus leaves for the Wars　　　　　　112
    War　　　　　　　　　　　　　　　　　119
    Homecoming　　　　　　　　　　　　　128

IV THE EMPIRE OF *COUPS D'ETAT*　　　　　133

V   BYZANTIUM AND THE WEST
    'The Greater Greece'　　　　　　　　　　162
    The Mission of My Lord Liudprand　　　　166

VI THE GREAT CATASTROPHE
    The Collapse of a Thousand Year Empire　　187
    The Capture and Sack of Constantinople by the Turks 193

INDEX　　　　　　　　　　　　　　　　　223

PLATES

1. The Pantocrator depicted in the apse of Monreale Cathedral — *frontispiece*
2. Theodosius receiving homage and gifts from the conquered The Empress Theodora — *facing page* 24
3. Theodora and her court Hagia Sophia, the Empress' Gallery — 25
4. The Golden Horn from Eyyub The Leander Tower — 36
5. Two Byzantine Curches: St John in Trullo; St Theodosea — 37
6. San Vitale, Ravenna Church of the Theotokos in Prinkipo — 68
7. Church of the Virgin Pammakaristos Church of St Irene Hagia Sophia — 69
8. Mosaic in the chancel of San Vitale, Ravenna Mosaic in St Apollinare Nuovo, Ravenna — 100
9. The resurrection of Lazarus Mask on the sarcophagus of a Byzantine Emperor — 101
10. A mystic relief on the wall of St Mark's, Venice The lion and the bull — 128
11. Mosaics from the old Monastery of the Holy Saviour in Chora, Byzantium — 129
12. The ambo of St Mark's, Venice The Byzantine ambo of Salerno Cathedral — 164
13. The dome of the Baptistry, St Mark's, Venice Interior Monreale Cathedral — 165
14. Fragments of the Imperial Palace The only one of the imperial palaces still standing — 196
15. The walls of Byzantium — 197

ILLUSTRATIONS IN TEXT

FIG.
1	Gold coin of 1160	page 17
2	Nicephorus Botaniates	18
3	Andronicus II Palaeologus	19
4	Ninth century patriarch	21
5	Tiara of Michael Palaeologus	22
6	An early Emperor in ceremonial dress	23
7	Court dress of high official	24
8	Medal with effigy of Alexius Commenus	28
9	Greek bishop of ninth century	30
10	Loeo III the Isaurian	31
11	The Empress Mary	32
12	Painting depicting a meal	35
13	An Empress	36
14	Grand Officer of the Empire	42
15	Three gold coins	46
16	Sixth century Christ	49
17	Sixth century Virgin and Child	50
18	The Emperor presiding over the games	56
19	Souls ascending, from eleventh century MS	65
20	Ninth century ascetics	66
21	Bisellium, a backless chair	70
22	Basil I	71
23	Ascension of Alexander	73
24	Mosaic from the Damascus Mosque	82
25	Two enamelled vases	87
26	Blue enamelled vase	88
27	Fragment of sixth century pottery	89
28	Coiffures	90
29	Silk fabric	91
30	A mosaic at Tyre	92
31	Hellenistic tapestry	94
32	Bronze door at Salerno	95

FIG.
33	Coin with effigy of Eudocia	page 96
34	Coin with effigy of Justinian II	97
35	Fabric preserved at Cluny	99
36	Fabric from the St Annott's chest	100
37	Reliquary	101
38	Fabric from Charlemagne's tomb	102
39	Oriental mercenary	108
40	Soldier of sixth and seventh centuries	109
41	Soldier of the Justinian guard	110
42	Grand Officer of the Empire	111
43	Altar	115
44	Soldier of the ninth and tenth centuries	117
45	Central part of ivory triptych	125
46	Lintel of a door at Dana	127
47	Coins of Tiberius Constantine and Justinian II	131
48	Decoration from a manuscript	136
49	Decoration from a manuscript	139
50	Christ as King	142
51	Various renderings of the Chrisma	148
52	Sixth century bishop	150
53	Sixth century priest	151
54	The Three Wise Men	152
55	The Adoration of the Magi	153
56	Detail from an ivory chest at Sens	156
57	Scene from Genesis in St Mark's	161
58	Cover of a reliquary at Limbourg	164
59	Sarcophagus at Ravenna	165
60	Eleventh century tapestry at Lyons	182
61	Capital from Hagia Sophia	187
62	Sculptured slab	192

I

THE KINGDOM OF CHRIST ON EARTH

Christ Incarnate

From the first, a stranger arriving in Byzantium would be struck by a series of strange and unusual facts. Sauntering through the town he might come across a monument inscribed 'Christos Basileus'—Christ, Emperor of Byzantium. When he was given gold coins at the bank he would see that most often they bore the head of Christ, crowned with the Imperial diadem. Icons on doorways showed Christ in unusual garments—those of the Emperor himself: the stemma on his head, scaramangion and debetesion on his body, and campagia upon his feet. The music of psalms and hymns might suddenly fill the street and a procession appear with an enormous cross at its head, crying rhythmically: 'Christ the Conqueror! Christ the Conqueror!' He might think he was witnessing a religious procession, though they were simply soldiers on parade.

If he were interested in legal matters he would find that laws were promulgated in the name of 'The Lord Jesus Christ, Our Master'. If he were present at a meeting of ambassadors he would see that by the side of the Imperial throne there was another, mysteriously empty, on which the Gospel was displayed, sometimes open, which none approached without bowing, moved and trembling. If he were to ask for an explanation, his informant, crossing himself, would whisper: 'It is the throne of Christ, our true Sovereign.'

Such indeed was the reason for all these singular features. The people of Byzantium strove to promote, among others as well as among themselves, the notion—so flattering to themselves—that the ruler of Byzantium was Christ himself. Looking for a people, the Son of God had

FIG. 1

Gold coin of 1160, with figure of Christ on the reverse (private collection) chosen them. 'Christ alone. Basileus'; thus could have begun and ended their chronology of kings.

Such megalomania had inevitable consequences: when the real sovereign is pure spirit, what can the emperor of flesh and blood in fact represent? He must necessarily be a materialization, a symbol: the materialization in our tangible world of an incorporeal substance, the symbol by which it can express itself here below. So it is that we find a State which had for its monarch neither a god nor a man, but an actor, a figurine. The Byzantine Empire was, in effect, nothing but the great scene of a spectacular drama, a mystery or a passion play, in which the consecrated dynast as the leading character played through the centuries the part of Christ. This helps to explain the strange customs which regulated the daily life of an emperor of Byzantium.

FIG. 2

Nicephorus Botaniates wearing 'the crown surmounted by a cross' (Bibliothèque Nationale, Paris)

To start with we might say that he dressed up, rather than dressed, having adopted the costume of an icon: over a kind of alb he wore a garment that was stiff like a cope and long like a chasuble, while on his head he wore a crown surmounted by a cross. Everywhere—on his arms and his shoulders, and dangling from his crown—were strings of precious stones and diamond rivieres. On Easter Sunday he even appeared surrounded by twelve apostles, his body swathed in white bands and his face as pale as death.

The palaces in which he lived were not homes, but theatrical sets reminiscent, naturally, of a church. Chapels outnumbered apartments and relics were hung on the walls, such as the Rod of Moses and the True Cross, and, on a background of gold, enormous images of Christ and the Theotokos, the Mother of God. Every month came processions of icons to renew the sanctity of the atmosphere.

Like those of an iconostasis, the doors of his residence opened

THE KINGDOM OF CHRIST ON EARTH

and closed at fixed hours; his throne was installed in an apse. Even his porter had been ordained as a priest. Quite naturally, the etiquette of his court was modelled on a religious ritual. He changed his attire constantly, in metamorphoses that were hidden from the laity, for he dressed and undressed behind a white veil, held by eunuchs. His garments were said to be divine, being, according to tradition, a gift of the angels to Constantine, and only the Church itself could be the vestiary—the sacristy, the altar or the vaults of St Sophia.

His receptions were not audiences, but revelations. He did not merely make an appearance, he manifested himself.

In the Sacred Palace the spectacle took place in a strange room, of perfectly octagonal shape, capped by an immense cupola; each wall was surmounted by an arch, so that the room consisted of eight apses. Many chandeliers hung from the ceiling. The furniture was strange too: golden lions, golden gryphons, golden birds perched on golden trees and, standing in a recess, reached by three porphyry steps, overhung by a canopy and veiled by purple fabrics, was the eighth wonder of the world, the Imperial throne. Everything was designed to disturb. Hardly had the intimidated visitor entered this metallic sanctuary than he was deafened by a terrible uproar. Some kind of machinery had been set in motion: beaks and mouths opened, the birds sang, the gryphons whistled and the lions roared; and when he had prostrated himself three times before the various porphyry circles and had looked around, he saw neither throne nor emperor. He had to raise his

FIG. 3

Andronicus II Palaeologus (1273–1322) wearing the tiara (from Du Cange's 'Historia Byzantina')

eyes very high to discover them suspended between the floor and the vault, raised above the earth by a mechanical device. Trying to talk would henceforth be futile: the idol was out of reach.

At the Magnaura Palace the reception was in the same style. The Basileus sat in the apse of the three-aisled Basilica on Solomon's throne, as rigid as his golden pedestal. The audience was a silent pantomime; all was done by gesture. The Emperor blinked, and the leading eunuch made a sign, itself hardly more noticeable: thus were orders given and conveyed. A sign of the cross from the Basileus marked the end of the interview, whereupon the visitors withdrew from his presence, walking backwards, with their arms crossed upon their chests. Just one word had been uttered: the *keleusate*—'if you please'—of the Master of Ceremonies.

To act Christ was, of course, a very exacting role. Every month there were more than thirty religious ceremonies and the Basileus had to figure prominently in each of them. Day after day, in a cloud of incense, Patriarch and Emperor toured the town, the former on a white donkey, the latter mounted upon an Arab stallion. One day they would celebrate the jubilee of a saint in a church, and on another they would be at the Pege Monastery to take the sacred bath. On Fridays they would attend together the miracle of Our Lady of Blachernae. And if at the Marian feasts the Emperor appeared with his head crowned with lilies, the Patriarch was first at the vintage festival. On this occasion the whole town—court, patricians, senators and people—made for the Asiatic coasts outside the walls, near the Hiereia Palace. While the dancing went on the factions sang hymns to the grapes. In an arbour decorated with bunches of grapes 'the two halves of God' engaged in mutual congratulations and offered one another baskets laden with juicy fruit, tasting and blessing the vintages. On Maundy Thursday they set out together to visit the homes for old people and there, to keep alive an old tradition, the Emperor washed the dirty feet of the inmates and kissed them.

Even in his private life the Basileus did not stop playing his part. His meals, for example, were full of subtle allusions to the Last Supper. After dessert he broke and blessed the bread and

THE KINGDOM OF CHRIST ON EARTH 21

raised the symbolic cup of wine to his lips. The number twelve—that of the apostles—haunted the ritual. There were twelve couches to each table and twelve tables faced his own. If six more tables were often added, it was only to accommodate the numerous guests whose attendance was required by etiquette. Ambassadors, high officials, 'officers the most noble, the most celebrated and the most eminent', bishops and hermits, 'princes of rhetoric', 'consuls of philosophy',[1] 'very discreet' lawyers, notaries, physicians, heads of hospitals, directors of orphanages and, at Christmas, the poorest of the poor—'our brothers in Christ'—crowded to his table. Prisoners of war were invited also, and on that day the Master of Ceremonies solemnly assured himself that all the dishes had been prepared in accordance with the foreign religion, without pork, for example, if they were Mohammedans.

In the antechamber the guests were stopped by an attendant. Before entering the banqueting hall, where, on a background of gold and mosaic, silver chains hung between columns of green marble and heavy chandeliers cast a dim light, they had to put on the ritual sash.

Nineteen couches, arranged in a semicircle, faced the empty throne. The Basileus had to keep his party waiting. At last, dressed in purple and with a white tiara upon his head, he came through a doorway at the end of the hall. Everyone bowed and, as though dazzled, shielded his face with his sleeves. The Master of Ceremonies hastened forward and helped 'the equal of the apostles' to ascend the three porphyry steps and take his place.

Now dishes appeared on moving trays. The Emperor himself

FIG. 4

Patriarch of the ninth century (from a painting on wood in the Firmin Didot Collection)

[1] University professors.

attended to his own dignitaries and favourites and each expressed his gratitude by rising and removing his sash.

Food was plentiful, though not excessive. There were hors-d'oeuvre with garos sauce[1]—caviare, olives, ginger, salad—followed by hot dishes, with game and poultry; the meal continued with cakes and sweets, washed down with Chios wines, and ended with fruit, offered in three huge chiselled bowls which were lowered from the ceiling and moved along by a special mechanism.

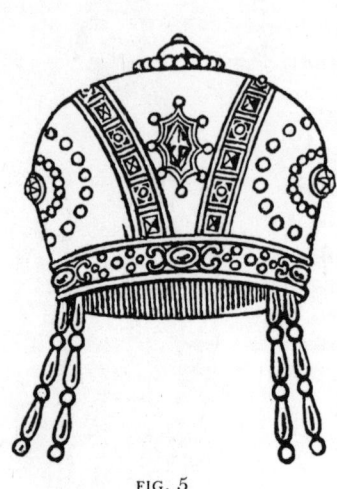

FIG. 5

Tiara of the Emperor Michael Palaeologus (from Du Cange's Dictionary)

The meal was embellished by varied attractions: music, miming and Greek dancing by the Greens and the Blues with the first course, readings from St John Chrysostom with the second, and Hindu jugglers and Chinese acrobats with the sweets.

Various compulsory interludes punctuated the dinner, such as the toast in Nauplian wine which everyone drank standing, with sash removed, to the health of the Emperor, and the washing of hands, prudently imposed by etiquette after the main dish.

As the entire meal was a religious ritual, the smallest lapse was punished by the severest penalties; thus decapitation awaited him who dropped a plate, while the guests who witnessed such a sacrilege must have their eyes put out. Need it be said that no one ever boasted of having witnessed such a mishap in the service?

Playing the part of Christ, however, quite obviously was not always onerous.

The Emperor inhabited in turn a dozen palaces of ethereal luxury. The principal one, the Sacred Palace, was a group of seven residences, with gardens containing pavilions, pergolas,

[1] A fish sauce famous in antiquity.

THE KINGDOM OF CHRIST ON EARTH

rose-water fountains, fish ponds and marble palestras. With its concert halls, museums, 'halls of beauty', 'love rooms', audience chambers, chapels and churches, twenty thousand servants were not too many.

His private apartments were a masterpiece of taste and refinement. Having passed many guard points and offices one saw it at last: a pavilion of exquisite grace, set amidst shady trees. Everywhere precious marbles and colourful mosaics vied with one another in splendour. The entrance, the great salon of the New Palace, built by Basil I, opened on to a colonnade of green marble and red onyx. Impressive murals, the work of the most celebrated artists, depicted the sovereign, his generals and outstanding events of his reign—'the Herculean labours of the Basileus', in the words of a contemporary—his solicitude for the welfare of his subjects, his activities on the battlefield, the God-granted victories.

The ceiling of the imperial bedchamber was a sky in which a green cross shone, surrounded by golden constellations. In the centre of the mosaic floor a peacock displayed its red plumage. In the corners, framed in green marble, were four eagles—the Imperial bird—with outspread wings. There were flower beds in mosaic along the bottom of each wall. Higher up the wall, in mosaic which stood out against a background of bright gold, the Imperial family in ceremonial dress was depicted: Basil, his wife Eudocia, their sons and daughters, each holding a holy book in one hand and making the sign of the cross with the other.

FIG. 6
An early emperor in ceremonial dress (Du Cange's 'Historia Byzantina')

In summer the Basileus occupied the Pearl apartments which, on two sides, looked out on to elevated gardens. Their golden vault was supported by four marble columns, and hunting scenes in mosaic decorated the panelled ceilings. In winter he used the Carian apartments which were protected by marble walls against the cold sea winds.

The apartments of the Empress were even more sumptuous. Her dressing room was paved with white and piously decorated with holy pictures. Her bedroom was called the room of *Mousikos*, that is, of Harmony, so enchanting were its colours and delicate its proportions. The floor of coloured marble resembled a field of flowers and the walls of porphyry, interspersed with green marble from Thessaly and white marble from Caria, were iridescent in the sun's rays. Further on was the Chamber of Love, the purple room where, by tradition, the infant basileis were born and from which they got the title of Porphyrogenite.

Everywhere ivory doors slid on silver tringles, great golden candelabra hung down and gold-embroidered tapestries harmonized with furniture encrusted with mother-of-pearl. The backcloth was of sloping flower gardens and hanging terraces, and the sheet of cobalt blue which was the bay, where, moving gently in the breeze against the blue eastern sky, was the Emperor's private fleet. . . .

King Midas was able to turn everything into gold; but the Basileus, the incarnation of Christ, by his touch made things sacred—letters, money, despatch boxes, stables. . . . An imperial message, written in red ink and bearing the golden seal must be placed first to the forehead, to the lips and only then respectfully opened. The court dress of the 30,000 members of the household could not be used in the outside world; it had to stay in the immense wardrobes of the Sacred Palace, for, metamorphosed by his gaze, it had become hierarchical. His investitures were

FIG. 7
Court dress of a high official of the tenth and eleventh centuries (from the Selected Works of John Chrysostom, Bibl. Nat., Paris)

PLATE 2. *Theodosius receiving homage and gifts from the conquered*

The Empress Theodora. A bust in the Castello Sforza at Milan

PLATE 3. *Theodora and her court. A mosaic in the chancel of San Vitale, Ravenna*

Hagia Sophia. The Empress' Gallery

sacraments. Like a communicant, the new official, having fasted on the previous day, received his charge on bended knees in front of the altar, a lighted candle in his hand. Since his person emitted a divine radiance, the nearer one approached him, the higher one rose in the hierarchy. Thus the dusting of his costume and the tickling of the soles of his feet were important functions.

Because he was divine, any abortive attempt against his person was regarded as a crime of *lèse-divinité* and punished as such by the severest measures—a successful attempt, on the other hand, would be viewed as the carrying out of God's will. A striking description of the tortures inflicted on an unsuccessful conspirator has been given by Rambaud in his book on tenth-century Byzantium. 'First', he writes, 'the culprit was put to torture to make him name his accomplices. Then in the Forum Amastrianon, or in the Funda of the Hippodrome, his feet or hands and his nose or ears were cut off, he was whipped with lashes beaded with lead, and his eyes were put out. He was then led around the amphitheatre or through the streets on a donkey. (In his biography Basil I is praised for modifying the punishment to the taking of only one eye and the cutting off of only one hand at a time. His biographer adds that Basil would have been even more merciful had it not been for considerations of State.) Under Michael III, when the enemies of his colleague Basil had been mutilated, they were set in a public place, each with a clay censer in the remaining hand in which sulphur was burnt instead of incense; they were then forced to cense one another. Next, for three days they were forced to beg in the streets, their eyes out, one hand cut off and the other held out for alms. Sometimes the usurper was beheaded before being whipped. Other times he was burnt alive like Phocas under Heraclius, like the maladroit would-be assassin of Leo VI, like the rebel Basil under Romanus I. Some, like one of the assassins of Michael III under his accomplice Basil I and the partisans of Dukas under the guardians of Constantine VII, were impaled. Other times simply the hair was cut or burnt off and the culprit shut up in a monastery; but often he was castrated as well. Almost always the criminal's entire family was enveloped in the disgrace: his wife shaven and imprisoned, his male children mutilated.'

Life might leave the Basileus, but not his radiance; for did not Christ rise from the tomb?

One day a young servant girl thoughtlessly spat through a window. Just at that time the coffin of the Empress Eudocia was passing through the street and received the saliva. The girl was put to death on the spot. What happened to the remains of Constantine is more typical still. When the great Emperor died, his son and co-regent, Constans, was far away. Who was to govern until he arrived? No one hesitated: obviously the embalmed remains of the deceased; to them the couriers read their messages, ministers explained their reports, the general staff revealed its plans, the Senate expressed its wishes, and the courtiers sought an audience. Thus, through an entire summer, autumn and winter, the Empire was ruled by a corpse.

As Christ was supposed to express himself through the Basileus, how could the Basileus ever be contradicted? The Byzantine Emperor succeeded eventually in gathering complete authority to himself.

Crowned and enthroned, the 'Autocrator' ruled over slaves (*douloï*). In him all powers were concentrated: executive, legislative, judicial and religious. He appointed and dismissed ministers, fixed taxation, commanded the armies, pronounced supreme judgment,[1] made and repealed laws, appointed or dismissed the Patriarch.

His power, theoretically universal, did not stop at the frontiers of the Empire. Like the Church, and for the same reasons, his sway was oecumenical.

He was often tempted, however, to mix sovereignty with caprice. There came a day when old Michael Stratioticus grew tired of the coiffures of the period and so formulated a law which made compulsory the cut of his young days. Theophilus was bald and could not bear the sight of an abundant crop of hair: consequently everyone had to shave his head. Leo VI had a weak stomach and could not digest the blood of animals; consequently no one in the Empire was allowed to partake of it.

The Senate, which had been so powerful in ancient Rome, was,

[1] The Imperial tribunal heard both first trial and appeals.

from the eighth century onwards, little more than a phantom. Even in the seventh century, its best period in the Eastern Empire, it was held in poor respect, for it was too easily entered: one had only to be wealthy or to hold an important public office. Henceforth, it was nothing but the solemn witness of great events: at the abdication of Theodosius, it was summoned to note the wealth of the treasury, and on the accession of Basil I to note its emptiness. On the occasion of the famous interview between Romanus I and the Bulgarian Tsar Simeon, it was called in merely to increase the number of attendants. Actually, it no longer had any official existence, for Leo VI had said: 'The Imperial Majesty having taken to itself the attributes of the Senate, the Senate is now useless.'

Equally, the people were no longer consulted; its representatives, the Circus factions, the Greens and the Blues, no longer played a public role; it was long since they had made emperors and shaken thrones. They no longer even exercised municipal functions, their civil and military committees had been dissolved long ago, and they were limited to taking part in parades. They no longer ranged themselves in battle order, but merely lined the streets for processions. Their pikes and shields no longer threatened the crown, but helped to control the crowd's enthusiasm. Not war-cries, but psalms, issued from their lips, with eyes fixed not upon the general's sabre but the conductor's baton. The people's sole activity was the making of epigrams and the composing of songs, though these could be caustic.

For instance, Michael Stratioticus had a passion for town-planning and caused much of the paving of Byzantium's streets to be taken up. But it was said that this was because, as a boy, Michael had lost a knuckle-bone he used in a game, and now he was trying to find it. Alexius Comnenus had gout and only his wife could massage him in a way that brought relief. So in almost every public show there would be a character, stiff-jointed, crown on head and weeping for his wife; shortly after, he was to be seen trussed up by a sturdy virago, shouting with pleasure under her vigorous rubbing. At sixty-five the Empress Zoë was still a virgin. She was amply to make up for it, it is true; meanwhile, to represent her in the pains of confinement was regarded as very funny. As for Justinian, how many couplets about his wife's past he had to endure!

Nearly all Byzantine emperors received nicknames, not all of them friendly. One of the Constantines had the misfortune to soil the baptismal font; for the rest of his life he was commonly known as 'Copronymus' ('The Pisser'). Michael had a well-

FIG. 8

Gold medal bearing on one side the effigy of Alexius Comnenus and on the other that of Christ (private collection)

known weakness for the bottle: he became for ever 'The Drunkard'. Another, who had been a ship's painter, was called 'The Caulker'.

From the sixth century onwards the town wits and gossips would meet under the balconies of the Royal Portico. Sitting there they would discuss everything—philosophy, politics, medicine, religion—air their views on current affairs and adopt attitudes which impressed and delighted the gaping crowd.

The emperors, however, did not take offence, but cleverly left this safety valve alone. The people might sing and banter, they thought, but they would obey.

A qualifying remark should be made at this point: however authoritarian the Basileus might be, his power was delegated. It was not in his own name that he acted, but in Christ's. He held a mandate. Consequently there were certain laws which he might not break, a kind of constitution which he must observe, and these laws and this constitution, as we shall see, gave to the Empire, in spite of everything, the aspect of a democracy.

A State with the Gospel for Constitution

What could be the constitution of a State that had Christ as its sovereign? There can only be one answer: the Gospel. In Byzantium, then, it was the Gospel that determined the structure of society and the position of the individual. From this it follows that the Byzantine Empire was essentially a democracy, an authoritarian one doubtless, but a democracy in the sense that the regime was equalitarian.

Firstly, there were no class or caste prejudices. The highest positions were open to all. Entry to the administration, the best ladder to success, was wide open to everyone. Advancement in it did not depend upon age or birth, but upon merit and ability. A particularly original feature was that any man who distinguished himself by some outstanding exploit quickly made his fortune. For the State would make him generous grants of land: behind the prosperity of the Phocas was the military prowess of Nicephorus the Elder, and behind that of the Lecapenus was the gallantry of a peasant ancestor called Theophylact the Insufferable. John the Orphanotrophos, the powerful minister of the Empress Zoë, was the brother-in-law of a stevedore. Psellos owed his immense wealth to the breadth of his learning, and the stable boy Philaraios owed his to an unprecedented circus trick in the Hippodrome, where he juggled with swords while standing on the back of a galloping horse. Within a few days, any poor, half-starved plaything of fortune could find himself the owner of several country estates adorned with gold and mosaics, and the centre of a court which included poets and saints, feeding thousands of slaves with bacon and chicken. Among hundreds of such cases there was that of Philaretus, once a poor serf, who became the owner of 1,000 horses, 1,200 sheep and 800 cattle, and at dinner frequently entertained 36 persons around an ivory table inlaid with gold.

In the struggle for life anyone might emerge with wealth and power; the poor and destitute were not forgotten in Byzantium; the town was full of homes for old people, shelters, charitable institutions, cheap boarding houses and, above all, hospitals.

The hospital founded in 372 by Bishop Basil was the size of a small town. Doctors and priests were there in large numbers. Orphans were taken in and taught a trade; even lepers were not turned away.

The community which Alexius Comnenus founded on the Golden Horn consisted of a number of institutions: an orphanage, a home for the blind and a military hospital. Together they cared for about 7,000 people.

The most representative was that of the Pantocrator, which was organized down to the last detail. Each sick person had a separate room, a bed-side rug, a pillow, a mattress, an eiderdown—double thickness in winter —a comb, a chamber pot, sponge, basin and slop pail. Baths were twice a week. In addition, each person was issued with two bath towels, two face towels, two bath-robes and, at Easter, a special allowance to buy soap. The cleanliness of the rooms was ensured by frequent sweeping out and the use of sawdust. Every morning inspectors made their rounds, asking about the quality of the food, for example, and listening attentively to complaints. The women were looked after in a separate wing by women doctors. Infectious cases were segregated and, thanks to an ingenious system of heating, enjoyed the most suitable temperature. New doctors were taught by qualified herbalists and a professor. A unique machine, of which everyone was very proud, cleaned the surgical instruments. The community was served by numerous kitchens, a dispensary, a bakery and a laundry.

FIG. 9

A Greek bishop of the ninth century (from a tenth century manuscript)

At the hospital attached to the Convent of World Redemption each patient kept his own plate, bowl, cup and pillow stuffed with wool. No bed was allowed to remain empty and women were admitted to its immense bathrooms on Wednesdays and Fridays.

To be a failure here below was no shame; for shall not the humblest here on earth be the most exalted in heaven? So Byzantium knew nothing of social arrogance.

The Basileus frequently entertained tramps at his table and

his door was never closed to anyone who wanted to enter. The following two stories illustrate this point.

One Sunday, as the Emperor Theophilus was leading a solemn procession, a working woman broke through the crowd and flung herself at the bridle of his horse. 'This horse belongs to me!' she cried. 'Your agents requisitioned it unjustly. Give it back to me!' She was not flung in prison; on the contrary, the Basileus dismounted, handed over the horse and continued his way on foot. From that time onwards, however, the ceremonial was slightly changed; as a precautionary measure the Emperor was accompanied henceforth by several changes of mount.

One day at the Circus two clowns appeared before the Emperor's box. They had some toy boats and were shouting at one another: 'Come on, try hard! Just swallow this boat.'—'It's no good, I can't do it.'—'Can't do it? The other day the palace prefect swallowed a huge galley, complete with cargo!'

The Emperor smiled and understood. He asked for details, summoned the accused man, confronted him with the plaintiffs and summoned witnesses. As soon as he was convinced of the official's guilt he ordered him to be burnt alive in full uniform. To everyone's delight this was done immediately in the Hippodrome.

Moreover, what reason had the Emperors for pride? So many of them were of the lowest origin. For in Byzantium anyone could become Basileus, regardless of rank, fortune and ancestry.

FIG. 10

Leo III the Isaurian (720–741), 'artisan and cheapjack' (private collection)

Leo I had been a butcher; people in Constantinople used to point out to one another the stall where he and his wife used to sell meat. Justin I was a poor swineherd from the Bederiana, who first appeared in the capital with bare feet and a pack on his back; one day, his nephew, haggard and in rags, also left the family village to join him; his name was Justinian. Phocas was a simple centurion, and Leo III the Isaurian was an odd job man. The parents of Leo V lived in the greatest poverty. Michael III was a servant, Basil I a peasant, Romanus Lecapenus one of the lowest in rank of petty officers in the navy.

All that was necessary for coronation was to be elected by Senate, army and people; and this procedure was never changed, even when in the course of time the need for a dynastic succession made itself felt. A system was then worked out which made some show of respect to democratic principles: during his own lifetime the Emperor elected his son. Thus for 24 years Leo III had for colleague his son, Copronymus, who had been crowned when one year old. The latter, in his turn, had his son Leo the Khazar as joint sovereign for 24 years of his 34-year reign.

The Basilissa, too, could be of humble origin; but she was expected to be beautiful. Hence the number of strange creatures who, one after the other, wore the purple gown: Khazars, singers, prostitutes, peasants from the Danube valley like Lupicina the cook and Theodora the bear-leader. How many humble workers became father-in-law to the Emperor!

Many pleasant stories have come down to us about these Imperial betrothals.

The Empress Irene decided one day that the time had come for her son to marry, so she sent messengers to the provinces with orders to bring back virgins of a certain height, figure, age and standard of beauty. The messengers set out. After much wandering some of them arrived one evening in a village of Paphlagonia very hard pressed for somewhere to sleep. They spotted a large, comfortable-looking house and knocked on the door. Finally an old man appeared and in reply to their request said, 'I have not much to offer you. For a long time, alas, I have beggared myself by giving. But I will do my best.' He called his wife and told her to prepare a meal. She grumbled: 'You have got us into such a plight that we have only one chicken left in the yard.'— 'Get on, don't worry,' the good man replied, 'God will provide.'

FIG. 11

The Empress Mary, wife of Nicephorus Botaniates, in ceremonial costume (Bibl. Nat., Paris)

THE KINGDOM OF CHRIST ON EARTH   33

The Almighty must have heard him, for by the time they had eaten dessert the envoys were feeling very well disposed and were congratulating their host on his health and vigour.

'Ah, thank you,' he replied. 'I am already a grandfather and, indeed, my three granddaughters are of an age to get married.'

The envoys, suddenly reminded of the object of their mission, gave a start. 'Old enough to get married? Where are they?'

The granddaughters were brought in and they were charming. One, Maria, was just the right age and height, and her figure met the required measurements also. The envoys were delighted and took the whole family to Constantinople. A dozen other candidates, all the daughters of aristocratic families and all very attractive, had already arrived. They stared disdainfully at the new arrival. She did not take offence, but proposed a treaty of alliance: let the one who was chosen look after the welfare of the others. The others laughed the proposal away.

'I can see the advantage for you,' replied one, 'for you have neither family nor fortune and, indeed, you have no chance. I am the richest and of the best family. There is no doubt that I shall become Empress.'

But it did not turn out like that. Maria, poor and of humble birth, became Basilissa. In Byzantium, as well as in fairy stories, princes married shepherdesses. . . .

After the death of Michael the Stammerer, Euphrozyme decided that her stepson Theophilus should marry, and had all the most celebrated beauties of the Empire assembled in the Pearl Triclinium. An apple was placed in the hand of the blushing young man for him to offer to the girl his heart chose. The young Paris was let loose among the petticoated battalion. He was intoxicated by exciting perfumes of the women and dazzled by their wonderful features. For some time he was too embarrassed to do anything. Then his eyes fell upon a young creature of radiant appearance; he approached her and wanted to pay her a compliment, but he was too confused to phrase his sentence well.

'It was your sex, you know, which brought unhappiness upon us.'

'But salvation, in the person of Jesus Christ, came to the world through a woman!'

This reply, prompt and much to the point, scattered the thoughts of the unhappy prince, who hastily put the apple into the hands of the nearest girl. Thus, beautiful Icasia lost the crown because she used a too ready tongue to a stammerer's son.

As all creatures are equal in the sight of God, strict equality between the sexes existed in Byzantium. While a girl, doubtless, led a rather sheltered life, and was not always free to choose her own husband, the married woman shared completely the life of her menfolk. Often, indeed, women dominated the family circle. The authority of Anna Dalassena, the mother of Alexius I, was notorious. At mealtimes Digenes Akritas respectfully awaited his mother and gave her the seat of honour, a chair, that is, while he was content to recline on a couch. To hold one's wife in seclusion was unpardonable. A certain *turmarch* (a military title) from Bizya was regarded as a very poor Christian for having relegated his wife to the gynaeceum on the occasion of a reception on the Sunday before Pentecost. Later, when she died as a result of his rough treatment, he was punished and his career ruined. Children often chose to take their mother's name. Thus the father of the Dalassenas was a man called Charon. This, incidentally, causes a great deal of difficulty in constructing the genealogies of the great Byzantine families.

Very revealing as regards this emancipation of women was the status of the Empress. She was the equal of her husband, she exercised absolute sovereignty, the incarnation of almighty God. And this quality did not come to her by virtue of her marriage, as a reflection, but of her own nature, from a true inner emanation. Ceremony bore this out. The Basilissa was crowned before the nuptial mass. Consecrated, she presented herself to the people; escorted by her chamberlains and ladies-in-waiting she slowly cleared a way for herself through guards, senators and patricians, and ascended the terrace from which she looked over the leaders of the State, the soldiers and the crown. One would look in vain for the Emperor. It was before her alone, glittering with embroidery, that the flags were dipped in salute, that the great and the humble prostrated themselves in the dust, that the factions offered their hymns.

When the Emperor Zeno died, his wife did not retire to the gynaeceum; rather, in full dress uniform, she went from the Palace to the Circus, accompanied by her leading officials and, standing in the Imperial box, spoke authoritatively to the assembled people. Under her presidency, she declared, the

FIG. 12

Fragments of a painting depicting a meal

Senate and the Supreme Council were going to meet together, with the approval of the army, to nominate a successor to the recently deceased Emperor. Almost immediately she returned to announce that she had been given this task. Whereupon the multitude shouted 'Yes! Yes! Keep the Imperial sovereignty, Ariadne Augusta!' And no Byzantine, from the sixth century onwards, when this event took place, ever found it at all strange. Diehl has given a careful description of the position of the

Basilissa.[1] 'She was the repository of authority; according to her wishes she could make an emperor, exercise power as a regent in the name of her children, or reign in her own right. At a time when the Teutonic West would have regarded with indignation the descent of power on the distaff side, Oriental Byzantium accepted without question a sovereign who, in her official acts, proudly inscribed herself "Irene, Basileus and Autocrator of the Romans".'

FIG. 13

An Empress, after an eighth century diptych preserved at Florence

Like other women, the Empress did not live in seclusion; indeed, she was constantly surrounded by men. Her coronation, even if it was rather less of a public spectacle than that of the Emperor—it took place in the Palace, not in St Sophia—required nevertheless the presence of the entire court. As she came out of the church the crowd cried, 'Welcome, Augusta, chosen by God' (not chosen by the Emperor). 'Welcome, Augusta, protected by God! Welcome to you who adorn the purple! Welcome to you, wanted by all!' Then everyone fell in behind her and accompanied her to the nuptial chamber. In the evening, at the wedding feast in the Triclinium Hall of the nineteen couches, she was surrounded by the leading personages of the Empire, 'the friends of the Basileus'.

Three days later when, according to custom, she went to bathe in the Magnaura Palace, huge crowds lined the route and followed her into the Palace gardens. What a strange ceremony! Attendants solemnly carried boxes of perfumes and brushes, caskets and vases containing toilet preparations; three

[1] Charles Diehl, *Figures Byzantines*.

PLATE 4.
The Golden Horn from Eyyub

...der Tower.
... of the points
...hich the chain
...ss the Golden
... was attached

PLATE 5.
Two Byzantine Churches:
(above)
St John in Trullo
(below)
St Theodosia

ladies-in-waiting held symbols of love in their hands, that is, red apples encrusted with pearls; mechanical organs played, the people applauded, mountebanks made bawdy remarks. At the door of the baths the parade stopped; the court dignitaries stood awaiting their sovereign's reappearance and finally with great pomp escorted her back to her apartments.

Very soon after she had given birth she would be visited by her immediate familiars. Sitting in the light of innumerable lamps, carefully wrapped in golden covers and surrounded by embroidered tapestries, she received the homage of thousands of visitors and watched to see that each one left a present in the cradle.

Numerous, too, were the receptions she held in the gynaeceum. The feast of the Brumalia in November, the survival of an old pagan celebration, brought an impressive number of guests to visit her. During the afternoon the women of her household received rich silken materials from her hands. In the evening there was a banquet; the choirs of St Sophia and of the Holy Apostles recited verses composed in her honour, comedians and clowns performed and representatives of the factions and grave court officials joined in a noisy torchlight dance.

The Basilissa also gave audience to princesses visiting Byzantium and these events were the occasion for banquets and the exchange of presents and courtesies. The way she discharged her duties as hostess affected the state of diplomatic relations and thus, to some extent, she played a part in the monarchy's foreign policy.

Her presence was required at all court festivities and at all important political ceremonies. 'Come forth, Empress of the Romans! Come forth, God-protected couple who add splendour to the crown! Shed light on your slaves! Gladden the hearts of your people!' Such were the acclamations of the crowd.

Finally the Basilissa held property of her own which she managed as she pleased, without consulting, or even telling, her husband. One day the Emperor Theophilus saw a particularly beautiful vessel enter port. Interested, he went down to the Golden Horn, visited the ship, was delighted with it and asked the name of its owner. To his amazement he was told that it belonged to the Empress. On board was a cargo of great value which his wife was hoping to sell without paying customs duty.

Indeed, there were no effective restrictions on her activities; even the ban on receiving men privately was not respected. Charles Diehl has written: 'Just as the ladies-in-waiting of the Empress were formally invested by the Basileus in the presence of all the men of the court, so the Basilissa received in her private apartments many high officials who did not belong to that reassuring category known by the name of "beardless officials".'

The following story illustrates this point very well. Anthimus, Patriarch of Constantinople, had been excommunicated by the Church as a heretic and condemned to exile by the Emperor. But the man disappeared and thorough search failed to find him; finally he was considered dead and the matter was dropped. Twelve years later the Basilissa Theodora died. Her husband Justinian went one day into the gynaeceum, when none other than the venerable priest stepped suddenly from a remote corner, quite at ease and in perfect health. For twelve years he had lived there without anyone knowing about it and, even more surprising, as Diehl maliciously pointed out, without Theodora ever giving away the secret.

Byzantium's democracy, however, was not of a secular nature; the Gospel was adopted as the constitution not from philosophical convictions, but because the City of God was believed to be organized along such lines. For, just as the Byzantines wanted their monarch to be the incarnation of the Son of God, they wanted their State to be the replica of the Kingdom of God. Consequently their entire political, social and economic structure was impregnated with divine significance. Divine was their law and order, and anyone who broke it was guilty of sacrilege. A law of Theophilus illustrates this point well; it said, in substance: 'He who assumes a rank which is not his, or lays false claim to an office, or assumes a dignity which is not due to him, may not put forward error as an excuse. Having blasphemed against the divine order, he will be punished for the crime of high treason.'

This attitude caused punishments to be extremely severe. A merchant whose measures were false had his hands cut off. A baker guilty of selling above the legal price was thrown into his own oven. A dishonest police official was burnt alive in the Hippodrome. Can one imagine worse punishment than the following one, inflicted upon the Basileus Andronicus, who was regarded as a usurper? For several days he was chained in the pillory, his head held in place by a great iron collar. The crowd beat him black and blue, broke his teeth with hammers, cut off a hand and hung it on a gallows. Then naked, half dead and starving he was tied on to a scabby and sick old camel in such a way that his head was under its tail; excrement from the sick animal dripped upon his face. In this way he was paraded through the streets. On the way a girl emptied a pail of boiling water on his face, women threw the contents of chamber pots over him, and one of his eyes was plucked out. He was still alive, however, and repeated 'Lord, have mercy on me! Why do you go on striking a broken reed?' At the Hippodrome he was strung up by his feet and the formal torture began. At last a sword was plunged into his entrails. As he died, he lifted a bleeding stump to his mouth; a nearby wit remarked, 'Look! He can't fatten himself on the blood of the people, so he's sucking his own!'

Such terrible executions sprang from the logic of the system: the greater the divinity of the institutions, one might say, the less human the punishments.

Other Religious Groups within the Empire

This picture of the Byzantine social order would not be complete without an examination of the position of non-Christians in the Empire: Jews and barbarian prisoners.

Contrary to what one might expect, the treatment meted out to the two groups was widely different; for an explanation we must look to the myth that Byzantium was Christ's own town. The Jews were held in very poor regard. To a court which intended to apply the principle of retaliation to a Christian who had murdered a Jew, a holy man exclaimed, 'Do you not know that the life of one Christian is worth that of seven Jews?' The shamefaced judges withdrew the sentence of death.

When Theodore in the seventh century was unable to find any other money-lender and turned to Abraham, his friends refused to stand surety for him. None would have anything to do with a deal in which a son of Israel was involved. And, be it noted, the loan agreed to by the Jew was free of interest.

The most sordid tasks were readily given to them, that of executioner for example. As many were not very skilful with their hands, a great deal of extra suffering was caused; the unhappy Romanus IV experienced this when his eyes were put out.

The excommunicated and the damned were buried in the Jewish cemetery. In legal matters their form of oath was regarded as ridiculous and vexing. This is how a judge had to administer the oath to a Jew in the eleventh century: 'Take off his belt, and replace it by one of thorns. Plunge him in the sea up to his neck, have him stretch forth his hand upon the water and repeat these words: "By the God who created Adam and Eve, who revealed the law of Moses, who has performed great miracles, who allowed the Israelites to cross the Red Sea with dry feet, who prepared food for them in the desert and gave them manna from heaven, I swear that I am speaking the truth and that I shall lie about nothing".' In the twelfth century it was even more striking. 'He must gird himself with thorns and enter the sea astride a water-skin saying, "By Barasa, Baraa, Adonaï, Eloï who caused the Israelites to walk across the Red Sea, who quenched their thirst by bringing water from the rocks, who gave them manna and quail to eat even though they had disobeyed and eaten the flesh of the pig; by the Law of Adonaï and by the thorns which gird my loins, by the name of the Lord of Sabaoth, I swear not falsely. If I swear falsely may the children of my loins be accursed, may I stumble into walls and fall like a blind man, may the earth open up and swallow me like Dathan and Abiron".'

Constantinople placed Jews in a ghetto: in the tenth century it was called Chalkoproteia and situated near the Golden Horn in the Pera district called Stenon. In all respects the Jews were second class citizens with diminished rights. They were barred from public office, could not own or deal in slaves, could not appropriate the soil of a church, could not go to law, could not bear witness against a Christian or marry one, all mixed unions being regarded as adultery and punished as such. Jews were not allowed in public baths or lodging houses. They had to pay a special tax, the nature of which was not fiscal but vexatious. A Jewish doctor was not allowed to ride a horse. Attempts to convert to their faith were officially forbidden and the law bore equally upon the missionary and the convert. The circumcision of a Christian was punishable by death if it concerned a child and by the confiscation of property and banishment if it concerned an adult. Reversion to Judaism was a crime for the apostate.

Thus the second Rome was far from following the tolerant policy of her predecessor, even though the Jews could not by any stretch of the imagination be regarded as a danger to the Empire. At the period of their greatest prosperity they numbered perhaps 15,000 in an empire of fifteen millions. They did not even excite economic jealousy, for in the East they were not rich: they had not monopolized money-lending at interest as they had in the West, for orthodoxy did not forbid the faithful to make their capital bear fruit. They were for the most part humble workers in industry, particularly the silk industry. If they were persecuted, it was on ideological grounds only: because their ancestors had killed Christ, the king of the realm, and because they refused to redeem themselves by embracing Christianity.

Quite different was the treatment meted out to barbarian prisoners of war, even though their first contact with the town was none too pleasant. Let us pause for a moment to conjure up the scene on a day when the victorious army arrived in the capital to make its triumphal march, with a long file of prisoners bringing up the rear. What an event that was! At dawn the heralds went to the four corners of the city to order a display of bunting and the sprinkling of scented water in the principal streets. Soon palaces, churches and houses were disappearing from sight, so heavily decked were they with leaves, laurel garlands and draperies. Balconies sparkled with gold and silver vessels, with candelabra and painted or sculptured diptyches. Ribbons of flaming colours streamed from the windows. Torches were lit though the sunlight was brilliant, and thousands of incense burners spread their intoxicating odours through the streets.

At first the thousands of captives were massed in close order in the midst of the booty. Later they would be taken to the Circus for the victory celebrations. At their feet gleamed the richest arms on a multi-coloured carpet of standards and flags. Farther on, beautiful Arab horses, tails and manes plaited, pranced and whinnied with excitement. Farther still were strange ungainly camels.

FIG. 14

Grand Officer of the Empire, bearing lance and shield

In spite of the early hour a vast crowd, composed of many nationalities, awaited the arrival of the victorious general. Many people were gaily dressed for the occasion; everywhere the crowd threatened to overspill but was held back, rather roughly, by soldiers of the Barbarian Guard and by the militiamen of the Factions. The Basileus was already in St Sophia, where he had arrived in procession on horseback, preceded by the great equerry, the *Protostrator*, who held the Imperial lance and flamoulon.[1] The Patriarch, too, had arrived, but mounted on an ass, and attended by his staff of priests. While hymns were sung to the Virgin Hypermatros, 'she who never forgets her flock', Basileus and Patriarch had exchanged the kiss of peace.

But where was the hero of the day, the victorious general? What was he doing? According to custom he had spent the night outside the city walls in camp with his soldiers. The town was now ready to receive him, and under the Golden Gate an official was waiting to crown him. At last a great shout rose to the skies. On foot he was making his way with difficulty through the enthusiastic crowds along the paved roads, his head crowned with

[1] A brightly coloured pennon.

laurel![1] He was making for St Sophia to bring to the scene of his triumph the two most eminent personalities in the Empire: Basileus and Patriarch.

And suddenly, amid the cheering crowd, the three moved forward together to the Circus; the tiers were crammed with people. The Domestic of the Eastern *Scholae*,[2] followed by the *Stratigos* on duty,[3] the *Turmarchs*[4] and other officers, ran into the arena for a last minute look at the prisoners to see that all is in order. At last, on the arms of two patricians, the Basileus appeared in the imperial tribune. Instantly a hundred thousand voices fell silent. All eyes were on him. Slowly, three times, he made the sign of the cross—in the centre, to the right over the Blues, to the left over the Greens—then sat on his golden throne. The master of ceremonies turned to him humbly and begged him to nod. He did so. Three resounding knocks were heard- the long awaited signal—and the show was on.

The leading Imperial chorister stood up, and in a slow, but marked rhythm began to recite the majestic verses of Byzantium's hymn of triumph:

> Let us sing to the Eternal God most high, for Pharaoh's chariots and his hosts hath he cast into the sea. The Eternal One is my strength and my God. He cast Pharaoh's chariots into the sea. Hail, oh King of the Romans, light of the Universe, to whom the Trinity has given victory. Incomparable soldier, defender and teacher of the world, subdue now all the nations with Christ's army.

The palace officials and the people made the responses and the true character of the victory became apparent: it was not only that of the Empire and its soldiers, but above all that of Christ and the true Faith.

But again, and suddenly, complete silence fell; the ceremony had reached its climax. The *Protonotary* flung himself upon the leader of the conquered, threw him to the ground and held him

[1] This of course is a description of the more usual 'triumphal entry on foot', and not of a 'triumphal mounted entry'.
[2] Title given to the Commander-in-Chief of the Eastern Army.
[3] Title given to the military commander of a region.
[4] Title given to the military commander of the 'turma' or sub-district.

there with his head against the feet of the Basileus who 'motionless . . . according to custom, strikes an attitude of haughty and cruel indifference'. Now the Emperor's red boot rested on the barbarian's head and the steel of his lance upon his neck. Then, while piles of lances and captured standards were roughly thrown down, the other prisoners were thrown face downwards to the ground, bellies in the dust. A brutal and sadistic spectacle. But all this was really only an act. In fact, captivity in Byzantium was quite pleasant.

After the ceremonies of triumph, whose ritual savagery was staged with the one object of impressing the crowd, the prisoners did not remain long at the feet of the Basileus; they were quickly raised up and invited to share the riches of the Empire. The chiefs were given estates, frequented the Court and took part in Palace festivals, games at the Circus, theological disputes and deer hunts. They went to the Zeuxippos baths, to be kneaded by clever masseurs, to the taverns to applaud the comic songs and the daring mimics, to the Church of the Holy Apostles to hear hymns, or to the cloisters to follow subtle discourses on dogma. Some would mix with wrestlers, dancers and charioteers; all came and went within the city as they wished. And so in the many pleasant public places, near the fountains, for example, and under the statues in the arcades, the sobriety of the Greek dress was relieved by many splashes of exotic and colourful costume.

These captives were even provided with places of worship appropriate to their religions. Thus the Saracens in Byzantium, the Christian town *par excellence*, enjoyed the use of a mosque—of a synagogue as it was then called—where prayers were said in the name of the Sultan.

Let a man only agree to become a Christian and he would immediately receive full citizenship. Honours, precedence and dignities would be within his reach, and also the hands of the most beautiful girls, if he was unmarried. The Emir Kouroupas, the conquered tyrant of Crete, could have entered the Senate, had he abjured. Indeed, his son Anemas did change his religion; he became a palace guard, and soon led his former enemies to victory.

How can we explain this tolerance of a degree unknown even to our so-called civilized times! The answer is that, dedicated as she was to the service of Christ, Byzantium was concerned less with conquest than with conversion. New territories were annexed only to help in the propagation of the True Faith. For the orthodox Byzantine the main task of the army was to break down barriers which stood in the way of the true religion. Wars had only one aim: to find a way to the heart, to make an opening through which the divine light could enter.

In any case, this was a clever policy, for after a while very few prisoners wanted to return to their cold mountains, to the primitive life they had left behind, and were won over for all time to the cause of Byzantium.

The Angels

To create a society in God's image, to set up celestial institutions, to treat prisoners according to the teachings of Christ—such acts, such achievements must surely command respect. And yet Byzantium was not impelled by high ideals alone; pride and megalomania also played their part. How intoxicating to be able to present oneself to the surrounding barbarian world as an extension on earth of the Kingdom of God, as part of God's Paradise! And what possibilities this offered of haughty disdain! In imitating Heaven, Byzantium showed her acceptance of adult behaviour; but she also demonstrated her immaturity.

Why did Byzantium use so much gold? Why were her five hundred cupola-crowned churches given a thick coating of gleaming metal, golden domes, golden icons? Why were gold engraving and the minting of coins the main industries in the streets? Why was Constantinople the world centre of the trade in gold, the place to which the civilized world brought its crude metal and from which it took it away worked? Why did the Basileus live in what might be called a cloud of gold? His court dress was interwoven with gold; his plates, his throne and even his toothpicks were of gold. Why? The answer is that in the Book of Revelations there is a passage which says that a heavenly

Jerusalem will open its gates unto the chosen people and that this Jerusalem will be entirely of gold. 'And he that talked with me had a golden reed to measure the city, and it was all of pure gold, like unto pure crystal.'

No statues were to be found in the churches, three dimensional art was ignored, if not actually held in disrepute. People

FIG. 15

Each emperor struck a gold medal bearing his own effigy: (top left) John II Comnenus and the Virgin; (right) Constantine X; (bottom left) Manuel I Comnenus (private collection)

were depicted only through such media as pictures, icons and mosaics, that is, without relief, as though they were abstract forms. The reason is that flesh does not live on into the eternal life, where all is spirit. Madonnas might have boys' legs, saints might widen from head to foot like a pyramid, strange animals might support thrones, and flowers unknown on earth might appear on ornaments. Why not? Byzantium was playing her part, that of the City of God, where only fantastic and supernatural beings were to be found.

Finally, if some men were castrated, if the Empire enjoyed the services of this rather unexpected class of 'beardless officials', there was but one reason: the angels, those important attendants around the throne of God, must be represented here below. Strange as it may seem, the eunuchs in Constantinople had no other *raison d'être*, for Byzantine women did not live in seclusion and there were no seraglios. It was not the Muslim world that gave them to the Christians, but the reverse; for when, from Byzantium, they reached the Ommayyad Arabs—from whom they eventually passed to the Turks—they at first did not know what to do with them.

And like the cherubim whom they claimed to represent (in church they sang a well-known anthem, 'We, the cherubim sing . . .') they veiled their faces as they approached their master. Like those of the cherubim their functions were to guide, to present, to transform, to transmit. They guided visitors towards the throne while supporting them with their shoulders, as though with wings; they presented to the Emperor the sacred insignia of the coronation; they transformed the earthly warrior who was about to reign into the image of Christ; they transmitted orders from the top to all parts of the hierarchy. Thus they occupied in the Empire a privileged position which they owed to the celestial quality of the part they played. Not only were the highest positions open to them, notes Galahad, but many were reserved for them alone.

If one wished to ensure a successful career for one's son, one had him castrated. He might then easily become a governor, ambassador, prime minister, *strategos*, admiral or Patriarch. Only one position would be closed to him, that of Basileus, for Christ was not an angel.[1]

The prominence of eunuchs in Byzantium, in number and position, led to a good deal of ribald comment amongst their enemies. The following story is told by Lebeau: 'The Greek Emperors had sent troops to help the Duke of Naples. Thibaut, Duke of Spoleto, won many advantages over them and took many prisoners whom he returned after having castrated them. His cruel jest was that it was to help them to get on in life, for they would now be held in high esteem at the Court of Constantinople. He told the unhappy men to assure their Emperor that he would do the same for as many others as possible. It was obvious that

---

[1] In view of the energy which most eunuchs displayed, doubt has been expressed as to whether they were castrated in the full sense, as indicated by the surgical term *membri ablatione*. Some historians incline to the view that they were semi-castrated in the way that does not rule out sexual potency.

he intended to keep his word. One day a woman whose husband had been taken prisoner entered his camp and tearfully asked to see the General. The Duke asked her why she was so distressed and she replied, "My Lord, I am astonished that a soldier with your reputation, once he has the men in his power, should amuse himself by making war on women." Thibaut replied that he had not heard of any prince making war on women since the time of the Amazons. "My Lord," replied the Greek woman, "could you commit a crueller act of war than to deprive us of children? When you make eunuchs of our men you mutilate us. I did not complain when you took our animals and goods. But you have struck a dreadful blow at some of my friends; when I heard that you were going to treat the new prisoners in the same way, I had to come to solicit the compassion of the conqueror." This woman's sincerity and simplicity so impressed the Duke and everyone present that her husband and all that she had lost were returned to her. As she was leaving the camp she was asked how she thought her husband should be treated if he were again taken prisoner under arms. She said, "He has eyes, a nose, hands and feet; those are things you can take from him if you think he deserves it, but leave him what belongs to me".'

Party Politics

Although Byzantium was dedicated to Christ, one should not conclude that everyday life in the Empire was morose or sanctimonious. In a hot climate, under a blazing sky, men lived passionately and in Constantinople as elsewhere, the average Byzantine citizen indulged in politics; but in a different kind of politics. For Byzantium was without earthly preoccupations; with eyes raised to heaven it aspired to resemble as closely as possible God's Kingdom on high. And this of course is where there might be grounds for dispute. Some would say, 'No, things are not like this up there,' and would demand reforms. Others would defend the *status quo* saying, 'Our copy is indeed the true copy.'

Participation in many of the quarrels—concerning the nature of Christ, the sex of the angels, the value of images, for example—required a detailed knowledge of the scriptures and other more abstruse sources. In Byzantium the man-in-the-street was able to discuss the Mysteries and the Reincarnation, the Essential Nature of Christ and the Trinity. Theology was a common topic in the theatre and at the work bench. Street loungers might argue about a passage in the New Testament or an article of faith. A difference in the interpretation of a verse might lead to a scuffle or a brawl, or perhaps to civil war.

In the fourth century Bishop Gregory of Nyssa wrote in amazement: 'Everywhere, in humble homes, in the streets, in the market-place, at street corners, one finds people talking about the most unexpected subjects. If I ask for my bill, the reply is a comment about the virgin birth; if I ask the price of bread, I am told that the Father is greater than the Son; when I ask whether my bath is ready, I am told that the Son was created from nothing.'

The famous quarrel about the nature of Christ—was He the equal of God (*homo-ousios*) or simply in God's image (*homoï-ousios*)?—caused trouble in the Empire over a period of eight centuries and led to the persecution, banishment and impoverishment of millions of men in three continents.

FIG. 16

Sixth century Christ in mosaic at St Apollinare Nuovo, Ravenna

Strange snatches of conversation were to be heard: 'The person of Christ divine?' one would exclaim. 'Pure idolatry! The Messiah was simply an inspired man, a messenger of God.' This was the Arian theory.

'Blasphemy towards our Creator and our faith,' the defender of the monophysite theory replied. 'Who could imagine a church whose central figure is not a God? There was nothing human about Our Lord. The divine spirit had finally absorbed his bodily substance.'

This brought the following retort: 'If you say that his body was some kind of ethereal phantom, what significance has his resurrection for us creatures of flesh and blood?'

FIG. 17

Sixth century Virgin and Child in mosaic at St Apollinare Nuovo, Ravenna

'Well then,' a third person would interpose, a disciple of Nestorius, 'can't these opposite views be reconciled? Why not regard the Saviour as a being of two aspects, human and divine? Jesus the mortal later becomes the divine *Logos*.'

But most people shook their heads for this would make Mary the mother of a mortal and not the mother of a God. And Mary was too much loved in Byzantium for this to be accepted.

There were naturally many other theories and variations.[1] The official attitude was quite open: 'Why bother about these things? These problems are too difficult for us. Why not regard it as a miracle and leave it at that!' But no one of course listened to such an unexciting view.

So strong were feelings in these matters that one's career might well depend on the position one adopted. If an ardent Nestorian took high office, Monophysite officials under him could expect dismissal, and so on. Because they were Arians, the Goths had no hope of ever founding a dynasty in Byzantium.

Even the soldiers had their choice to make; their posting and

---

[1] If Justinian had only Manicheans, Monophysites and Nestorians to deal with, Heraclius had to manage in addition Syrian Monophysites and Neo-Severianists. Alexius Comnenus had on his hands the Paulicians, Bogomiles, Sabellians, Adoptionists, Massalians, Marcionites, Montanists and others besides.

promotion might well depend upon their interpretation of the Gospel. For the Empire had consigned whole communities of heretics to its frontiers: a legion of Paulicians, a regiment of Monophysites, a detachment of Bogomiles, etc.[1]

The first civil war of religious origin was hardly over before a second and similar one broke out. Should images be allowed? And on this point of canon law the population was divided into two camps; the women were to be found in one—need one say which?—and the soldiers in the other.

Here again there were solemn arguments on both sides. 'To make images,' thundered the iconoclasts, 'is to counteract the divine spirit, to reduce it to the material plane. To worship them is to fall back into paganism, to reduce the saints to something resembling the ancient gods.' Epiphanius of Cyprus declared: 'A Christian should not find his soul through the medium of his eyes or the straying of his senses.'

'But,' replied the iconodules, 'if Christ is God by virtue of his father, he is a man through his mother; to prohibit pictures of him is to deny his mother and to abandon hope of atonement. In any case, could God be the enemy of images when he made us in his image? When we contemplate the image, we are not worshipping the material, but the creative spirit.'

It was the Basileus Leo the Isaurian who, in exasperation, brought the matter to a head. He was exasperated because invariably the saints got the credit for his victories, because so much of the fruits of conquest had to be handed over to the church to enrich the altars. One fine night in 794 he had faggots stacked round the Academy of Sciences and surreptitiously set fire to it. In a few minutes 30,000 volumes, many of them irreplaceable—notably an edition of Homer on lizard skin—perished in the flames, together with the 13 scholars who had assembled them.

The struggle was marked by many vicissitudes, some comic, some tragic. One morning, when they went to divine service,

---

[1] From the Bogomile doctrine there came the heresy—the Albigensian heresy—which caused so much bloodshed. As it had repercussions in medieval France, and as it is interesting in itself, we have thought it worth while to set down some remarks about it in an appendix to this chapter.

the faithful could hardly recognize the Church of the Holy Apostles; it seemed to have been turned into a vegetable market, for on the walls, instead of the usual effigies of saints, there were crude drawings of carrots, turnips and cauliflowers. One afternoon Michael Lachanodracon, the elderly and most ferocious adviser of Constantine Copronymus, shepherded thousands of monks and nuns into the arena of the Circus and ordered them, under pain of having their eyes put out, to pair off there and then. 'Byzantium needs soldiers, not idolaters,' he shouted. Nevertheless, many preferred the bliss of martyrdom to the pleasures of the flesh. Soon, to avoid mutilation and torture, more than 60,000 priests, monks and nuns sought refuge in the mountains or in Southern Italy. Here and there women suspected of concealing reliquaries about their persons were hunted and cut down by the sword and their remains kicked into streams. Monks who had been scalped by soldiers would try to close the gaping wound with their beloved images. Others had their beards set alight. On the other hand, soldiers were lynched, St Sophia was invaded and the Patriarch stoned to death by a crowd of women.

But a war of soldiers against women is not fought on equal terms. While Constantine Copronymus fulminated against iconodules, his daughter Anthusa worshipped her favourite saints in the Sacred Palace, under his own roof. Theophilus was a convinced iconoclast, but he could not prevent his mother from retaining some wonderful 'dolls' with which she amused her grandchildren during meals; nor could he prevent his wife from hiding others in the gynaeceum, or pressing them fervently to forehead and breast.

On February 19, 843, after a century and a half of struggle which had been marked by more than the usual amount of treachery and brutality, the war ended in victory for the iconodules. Victory was celebrated by a solemn Te Deum in the Church of St Mary Blachernae, and on the following day by an imposing procession of images and candles. The event is still commemorated by the Greek Orthodox Church.

The outcome of the struggle was to have extremely important repercussions for the future of the Empire. Along the Syrian frontiers lived nearly six million convinced iconoclasts; soon they would welcome Islam, the enemy of images, as a liberator. Thus the loss of many provinces was the price Byzantium paid for the sensual enjoyment of divinity.

The Hippodrome—an Ersatz Forum

However hard one tried, one could not go on for ever discovering material for controversy in the New Testament. If one is of an ardent nature, one must look for something else. Modern man with his earthly ideals finds fuel for his passions in *Das Kapital, Mein Kampf* and a hundred other profane Bibles. Not as richly provided, the Byzantine had to resort to sham politics. He discovered the Circus, the Hippodrome.

Actually it was not so much a discovery as an adaptation. The Hippodrome already existed in Rome, but here in Constantinople it took on a different style and meaning; there were no gladiators or wild animals or blood in the arena, but two rival clubs—the factions—which competed in chariot races. They were known as the Greens and the Blues from the colours they displayed.[1] The Byzantine betted heavily, not so much in the hope of monetary gain as for the satisfaction of taking sides. He plumped for Green or Blue as a modern elector votes Left or Right; the race course yielded the emotion that the voter experiences when the results are counted after an election, and the factions faced one another with as much hostility as do two extreme political parties.

There was of course no economic or political or any other kind of reality behind all this excitement. The Byzantine was Green or Blue for the flimsiest reason, such as a preference for a colour or the element it represented. But, he would say, *what* one desires matters little, the thing is to desire. And he shouted,

---

[1] Originally there were four factions: Greens representing the earth, Blues the sea, Whites the air, and Reds fire; but after a short time the Whites were absorbed by the Blues, and the Reds by the Greens.

screamed and lost his temper for the pleasure of it, for the intoxication of taking sides.[1]

In his remarkable *Etudes sur l'histoire Byzantine*, Rambaud has painted an amusing picture of the state of mind of the racegoer at Constantinople. 'With us,' he writes, 'what interests most of the spectators are the bets they have put on. In Constantinople the poor devil of a plebeian, the Bosphorus boatman, the shipyard worker of the Golden Horn, had no money to put down; the stake was his own self-esteem. Once he had taken his own seat on an appropriate tier in the Hippodrome, and sported his green sash, the defeat of the Blues was a triumph for him personally, their victory a heart-breaking event. Let his driver fall from the chariot near the winning post perhaps, or his side experience defeat, and his sorrow and humiliation are boundless. How can he walk down his own street, pass his neighbour's shop, enter his own home even? That green sign, once respected by the Emperor himself, is going to make him the target for jibes and insults from half the street loungers in Constantinople. If, on the other hand, his favourite driver pulls it off, he will be in the eyes of his supporters a greater man than the Caliph of Baghdad and the exulting down-and-out will stride triumphantly down the grand avenues with his colour proudly displayed and head held high, intoxicated by the flattering comments of the crowd.'

Thus, in spite of appearances the spectacle had lost nothing of its violence since Roman times. Battles were fought no longer in the arena but amongst the spectators during the interval and after the races. Mercenaries were no longer hired for bloodshed: people killed one another. Now the citizen himself acted in the show and nothing was lost in the excitement. The Emperor's guards might intervene with sabre, whip and baton, but they could not always separate adversaries who had set upon one another. They might be vigilant but they could not prevent high-spirited Blues from tossing some Green into the Bosphorus,

---

[1] Some writers contend that the factions represented religious or social groups or symbolized their aspirations. According to them, it would appear that the Greens made themselves the champions of the lower social groups and the Blues the champions of the higher (see amongst others an article entitled 'Le Pruple de Constantinople' by Manoglovic in Volume XI of *Byzantion*). This thesis, however, has been attacked quite recently by Mr Carcopino.

THE KINGDOM OF CHRIST ON EARTH

sewn up in a leather bag. Sometimes they themselves added to the loss of life as on the day when, in suppressing a fight between the Factions, they left 40,000 bodies in the Circus. In the reign of Justinian, Chronicius made the following observation: 'Racing seems to lead to anger rather than joy and it has already been the ruin of several important towns. It leads to the squandering of money, to crime and death. Men put the interests of their team higher than those of family, home or country. Both men and women are seized by a kind of madness and, indeed, racing is a very widespread sickness of the spirit.'

Every town had its hippodrome, the scene of competition between the Factions. The local clubs maintained close contact with the club in the capital, so that a real freemasonry of concentrated action existed throughout the Empire. When an Isaurian count savagely repressed a riot started by the Blues in Tarsus, the Constantinople 'lodge' was immediately informed and delegates approached Justinian to demand his punishment. The Emperor refused to act, for—and this is a point of difference between Rome and Byzantium—he must remain above the strife.[1] Still intent on revenge, the Blues of Tarsus lay in wait for him outside his own palace and struck him down.

The Hippodrome, however, was more than a racecourse: it was a political arena at the very centre of public life. The driver, who was selected immediately before each race, was not the anonymous member of a team, but the leader of a party. A successful driver received honours which in our day are reserved for famous statesmen. His statue would probably be erected in the Hippodrome or even in the square, next to that of the Emperor. Flattering lines were engraved on the pedestals: 'Anchisos is loved by Venus, Endymion is the darling of Diana, Porphyrius the favourite of victory.' Has any head of State ever received an epitaph comparable with the following? 'When in the course of time Nature brought forth Porphyrius, she said, with those lips which cannot lie, My task is complete, I can do no more, for all that I had of grace I have given to Porphyrius.'

In the most distant provinces of the Empire the name of the Basileus might be unknown, but everyone had heard of Caliopus,

---

[1] 'To the outside world a sovereign, to his own country a saint, he must remain above party.' Galahad, *op. cit.*

FIG. 18

The Emperor presiding over the games at the circus (from an ivory)

Uranius, Icarius, Anatellon, Olympius, Epaphroditis and other drivers whose chariots had several times been first past the winning post.

Thus, in spite of appearances, the people had preserved their ancient political rights. The right of assembly? As there was no Forum, they met in the Circus, a hundred thousand at a time. The vote? They selected not tribunes, consuls or magistrates, but charioteers. Freedom of expression? They could shout and howl, cheer and insult colours, chariots and horses as much as they liked. The right to revolt? As a result of quarrels arising out of incidents on the racecourse, the throne was shaken more than once.

For all these reasons the authorities took precautions.

Each charioteer was nominated by the Basileus, and the warrant signed in royal red, the belt and the silk embroidered cap were not handed over before the most solemn guarantees had been secured.

The Basileus nominated the leaders of the Factions also and announced the opening day of the Hippodrome much as certain present-day constitutional monarchs have kept the right to summon and dismiss Parliament or to choose its President.

The Emperor attended the games armed from head to foot. Imperial guards were stationed all round his box, which resembled less a tribune than a fort. It stood on columns high above the arena and was surrounded by walls and battlements. There were no exterior steps. It could have held out against a siege, for it was connected to, and really was part of, the Sacred Palace. To reach it the Emperor had no need to leave his residence, but went through his own gardens and marble-paved courtyards, along galleries and up a winding staircase. In his box he sat upon a throne surrounded by eunuchs, some of whom carried fans, while others carried swords.

The Empress was even more closely protected. 'Invisible yet present,' she saw the spectacle from St Stephens, a chapel of retirement built by Constantine between the Sacred Palace and the Tribune Palace. Thus her box was nothing less than the galleries and windows of a sanctuary; the Church became a branch of the theatre.

Not only the Empress, but the contestants had to be protected from the possible excesses of the crowd; for excited partisans were capable of the worst follies. Railings separated the arena from the tiers of seats. In earlier days a ditch, called the euripus because it symbolized the ocean which encircled the earth, ran round the arena. In time the water disappeared, but the name remained to describe that part of the track nearest to the spectators, which was patrolled by the Byzantine policemen, the *cursores*, batons in hand.

The Hippodrome had another, subsidiary attraction: it was the place where criminals were punished. There prisoners were beheaded and branded, eyes were burnt out, noses and ears cut off. It was in the Hippodrome that the Emperor Andronicus I underwent his terrible punishment, there in the reign of

Constantine Copronymus that monks and nuns had to copulate *en masse* to escape being blinded, that iconodule patriarchs were paraded sitting back to front on donkeys, that the illustrious Manichean doctor who argued theology with the Emperor Alexius Comnenus (and was unwise enough not to let himself be won over) was burnt alive.

We may begin to understand then the popularity of the Hippodrome. Many stories have come down to us which illustrate it. A certain landowner, in spite of entreaties and threats, had refused to give up certain property to the Emperor Justinian. The stubborn man had turned down a fortune, put up with prison and resisted hunger. He was despaired of, when the palace prefect had an inspiration. He was sent to jail again, and while he was there races were announced. Fearful of missing them, he held out no longer, but instantly surrendered his patrimony at a ridiculous price. Another landowner had to be promised a hereditary seat in the amphitheatre together with a display of Imperial honours upon his arrival in the stand. These honours, however, were to be rendered to his back and not to his face. This led to a piece of horseplay, as, through centuries, the crowd never failed to greet the descendants of this megalomaniac racegoer with jeers and exaggerated bows.

One day Michael III was taking part in a race in the hemicycle when messengers brought him dire news: a chain of beacon fires from the boundaries of the Empire to the gates of Constantinople announced the defeat of the army on the banks of the Euphrates. Did he withdraw hastily from the contest? Certainly not. He ordered the extinction of the bothersome beacons and to the delight of the crowd continued to lead his team.

The Hippodrome! For us, heirs of the humanists that we are, the name evokes quite different emotions. In the Hippodrome were to be found the splendours of classical art: jewels of ancient Greece, treasures from the time of Phidias, Pericles, Lysippus; sombre idols from remote centuries. Byzantium had amassed them up in the top tier in the porticos like an attic full of souvenirs. For of what use were they to Byzantium, that most Christian of towns?

As Rambaud[1] has feelingly written: 'There were palladiums

---
[1] Rambaud, *Etudes sur l'histoire byzantine: l'Hippodrome à Constantinople.*

by the hundred and protecting spirits and the souls of cities in bronze . . . there were statues of gods who in times gone by, in the shades of their own sanctuaries, had received entire provinces in pilgrimage, who had performed miracles and seen the offerings of worshippers pile up at their feet in clouds of incense, which had been stained by the blood of human victims, spattered with the blood of young Laconians scourged on their altars, and who had brought down the thunderbolt upon the heads of Brennus' Gauls. And there they were, in rows, lined up like common statues, and the indifferent crowd seemed to have no idea that they were rubbing shoulders with the gods.'

In this medley of treasures the grotesque and the sinister and the beautiful lay side by side. There were Hercules and Helen, flanked by dwarfs; Mars and Venus stood by the hunchback Formilianus. As all these things were the work of heathens, the devoutly Christian Byzantine was certain that they possessed all kinds of evil powers. One ill-shapen figure was reputed to devour men and beget beasts. A bronze eunuch bore a menacing inscription on his chest: 'He who moves me will die strangled.' It had been noticed that there were terrible earth tremors whenever the statue of Phidalia was moved. Once a year a great bronze bull roared and on each occasion a major calamity befell the town. One day, while the philosopher Asclepiodorus was studying the mysterious inscriptions on a statue of particularly sorrowful appearance, he fell into a profound melancholy. 'No, your Majesty,' he replied to the Emperor Athanasius, who was curious and disturbed, 'permit me not to answer your question. It were better so. Would to God I knew not what I now know.'

On the Spina there was a famous bronze column formed of three entwined reptiles with heads outstretched, which was said to communicate with evil spirits. A sad reputation for a monument of so respectable a background! For it was none other than the famous bronze 'dragon' minted out of the spoils of Xerxes' army, consecrated by the Spartan Pausanius in the temple of Apollo at Delphi, after the battle of Plataea. One could still read the names of the 36 hoplites which had furnished their contingents, from the little town of Mycenae with its 80 men to the powerful Sparta with its 40,000. Everyone in Byzantium regarded it with horror and fear, in spite of the wine, the milk and hydromel which an ingenious hydraulic system caused to flow from its mouths.

Consequently it had a career of many ups and downs. One night during the reign of the Emperor Theophilus, the Patriarch of Constantinople in great secrecy led three men to the Hippodrome. The men had hammers. After the monster had been exorcized by a powerful formula, the Patriarch ordered his servants to knock its three heads off. They managed to remove only two. It was left to a Turkish sultan—Mahomet II, Murad IV or Suleiman the Magnificent—to complete the work. He knocked off the third with one blow of his mace. And then, what a surprise! Constantinople began to swarm with serpents and it was realized too late that the dragon had been a friendly guardian.

The average Byzantine cared little for these treasures; at the most he would cross himself and hurry on. The Circus for him was the place where one shouted and screamed and cursed to one's heart's content.

Let us look at the crowd that had begun to assemble on the day before the races, for the spectators liked watching the last minute preparations. The staff was testing the barriers, examining the chariots, levelling the arena with new sand, spreading cedar sawdust and setting out the urns from which the names of the fortunate men who were to be on the inside, as well as the starting positions, would be drawn. All this took time, too much time in the opinion of the crowd, which urged the staff on with jeers and catcalls.

And the crowd was indeed a motley one, including as it did: craftsmen of Constantinople in their best clothes, Thracian peasants ground down by taxation, mountain dwellers from the Balkans, armed to the teeth, richly ostentatious pirates from the Archipelago, foreign merchants attracted by favourable tariffs, Hungarians whose dress tinkled with little golden bells, Varangians adorned with furs and silks, Bulgarians with shaven heads, western Franks, Arabs with flowing dress from Egypt, Syria or Sicily, Khazars, Croatians, Armenians.

Byzantium, indeed, was far too hospitable! How many of these barbarians, coming as guests, considered the possibility of returning as conquerors, as from the top of the Hippodrome they surveyed with covetous eyes the breathtaking panorama of silver roofs, gilded domes, broad avenues lined with marble columns and ancient trees, bronze columns, bronze-doored palaces and the majestic domes of St Sophia reaching to the skies!

Certain privileged people had reserved seats and need not arrive until the last moment. Such were the court dignitaries and foreign ambassadors who took up places not far from the Emperor under the great silk awning which moved gently in the breeze from the Bosphorus; such also were the members of the clubs, whose seats were in the tiers nearest the arena, Blues to the right, Greens to the left. The next day their light, purple-striped tunics and their team sashes would be soaked in sweat, and that short dagger and the staff surmounted by a crescent would perhaps be stained with blood.

As darkness fell, no one left the amphitheatre, no one was going to run the risk of losing his place.

As the great day dawned, all life outside the Circus had come to a halt: workshops, shops, dockyards, all were closed.

Suddenly there was a great deal of movement on the side nearer the Palace. A wave of flags, standards and guards in gilded breast-plates came on to the imposing terrace bordering the Palace boxes and standing above the arena like the Greek letter π, from which it took its name. Rostrums to right and left had filled up and finally the Basileus himself appeared. He was wearing his crown, in one hand he carried the sceptre and in the other he held the corner of his mantle, which was gathered up by a eunuch.

Three times the Basileus made the sign of the cross: to the centre, to the right over the Blues and to his left over the Greens. A thunder of applause broke out and the sound of organs filled the amphitheatre. The songs of the Factions arose, then suddenly all was quiet. The signal was awaited.

It was given and instantly at ground level, immediately under the royal box, four gates were flung open and four chariots drawn by four swift coursers rushed forward. The standing drivers, with bare arms and chests, with caps the colour of their Factions, daggers in their belts and whips between their teeth, and with the reins in their hands, seemed about to fly. The race began. Before returning to the start, which was also the finish, the light two-wheeled chariots made ten, fifteen or twenty 400-

yard circuits up one side of the arena and down the other. At each end was a triangle called the *meta*,[1] and there accidents were frequent. A horse might fall and its chariot swing out of line and overturn; those following crashed into it and in a few seconds there was a bloody pile of men and horses.

The drivers lean forward with knees braced, the harness is straining, one chariot overtakes another in a cloud of sand, the horses leaping forward foaming at the mouth, enveloped by the whip. And all the time the Factions sing their songs, shout their cries and mutter their prayers. 'Oh God,' said that of the Blues, 'protect the Emperor, protect the magistrates, protect our masters, protect our Empress and her children, protect the prefect and, oh God, protect Olympios, protect Anatellon! Give them victory, grant victory to the Veneti! Mother of God, let them be victorious that the Empire may be filled with joy, that we may dance the dance of triumph! Jesus is our protector! Victory for the Blues! We win, and the Emperor and his army will gain victories, there will be abundance in the towns of the Romans. May the divinity eternally grant triumph and glory to the Blues! Victory to the Autocrator, to the Empire, to the Veneti!'

Each race lasted about a quarter of an hour. They followed one another at a faster and faster pace, separated only by the crowning of the victor. After the fourth race came the interval during which there were all kinds of entertainments. There were exhibitions of strange animals and acrobatic feats. Clowns performed and dwarfs waddled about. Animal tamers paraded gilded crocodiles on leads. One Italian adventurer had great success by showing his clever dog, which from a circle of people could pick out the greediest, the most vicious and the most generous, could bring rings back to their owners and place medallions of the emperors in order. Often, too, spectators got down into the arena to play at horses and chariots: one took whip and reins, the other put the bit between his teeth and off they went, to see which of the various pairs could get home first. This little frolic was so highly appreciated that the Emperor Constantine VII solemnly noted it in his Book of Ceremonies.

[1] The one nearer the Imperial rostrum was known as the Blues' *meta* and the other as the Greens'.

At other times, to celebrate certain feasts, in the manner of Dionisiades of Eleusis, the leaders of the Factions, splitting their sides with laughter, engaged in sham fight, overwhelming one another with rehearsed insults and vulgar remarks. The Byzantine enjoyed it all immensely. The possibility of accidents made him particularly appreciative of the work of tight-rope walkers. One day with delicious horror he saw an acrobat at the very summit of the Great Obelisk stagger and then fall; he hit the ground with such force that all his bones were broken and he was forced deep into the sand. Such mishaps were frequent. In the course of a tour one group of gymnasts had lost half its members before it had returned to Byzantium.

These diversions brought the morning session to an end, but there would be more races in the afternoon.

Meanwhile one must eat. Leaving the Hippodrome was out of the question, so everyone unpacked his food on the spot; dried meat, salted fish, cooked peas, water melons, lemons and oranges were favourite items. Frequently the Emperor provided a meal and on such occasions eunuchs heaped huge piles of food at the foot of the *spina*—hams, fruit and vegetables—and, plunging into the arena, everyone fell upon the pyramids of good things. Sometimes a great quantity of dried fish was carted out and emptied on to the track. Of course, these victuals could not stand comparison with the Roman orgies. 'They hardly recall,' says Rambaud, 'the fabulous *congiaria* which Caesar in celebration of his victories, offered the Roman people seated around 40,000 tables, when nothing seemed good enough for the sovereign people, when the best wines of Greece and Sicily were generously dispensed to labourers and prisoners.' The reason for this relative frugality was obvious: the Eastern Empire was by no means as wealthy as its predecessor; moreover orthodox Byzantium was, officially at any rate, sober in its habits. It was more nearly typified by the Patriarch John, nicknamed the Faster, than by the gourmand Vitellius.

But eating was not the main business on hand. The people always finished their snack quickly, and then felt that the Basileus stayed too long, recalling him with songs that became less and less respectful. One day in the reign of Phocas, a rough old soldier, they had cause to regret this. After respectful invocations—'Arise, oh Imperial Sun! Rise and come forth!'—the Factions were soon shouting 'Come on, you've had too many bottles already. You're already seeing double!' The tyrant then let loose his guard; heads, noses and ears were cut off, and there was great slaughter. A few years later the same crowd had the intense satisfaction of seeing Phocas roasted alive in the bronze bull, on the orders of his successor, Heraclius.

The Empire of Miracles and Palmistry

In the fifth century Byzantium was visited by a terrible epidemic which took a particularly heavy toll of the working people. Surprised by this fact, a doctor made inquiries and discovered the cause: their cramped and underground dwellings lacked air. He hastened to advise the authorities. The result was instantaneous: everyone choked with indignation. Unhealthy conditions causing death? What an improper thing to say! God, and God alone, determined the hour of death. When, some time later, the doctor died of the infection, a victim of his own devotion, Heaven was praised for having punished his blasphemy.

Every Saturday evening the square in front of the Church of St John the Baptist in Byzantium was crowded with people; all around stood a multitude of cripples, their lower abdomens wrapped in bandages. They had struggled from every quarter of the Empire; they were suffering from disorders of the genital organs and had come to consult St Artemius, the famous specialist in such diseases. From the heavenly saint they expected healing. It was enough to dream about him by night to recover one's health. And as night fell each one dragged his mattress as near as possible to the altar and then conscientiously settled down to sleep. Delicacy forbade St Artemius to treat female patients directly and so he had a woman colleague, St Febronia. This was not merely an expression of the simple credulity of the poor and humble, but the recognized treatment, the only remedy recommended by the medical faculty, for venereal diseases.

THE KINGDOM OF CHRIST ON EARTH 65

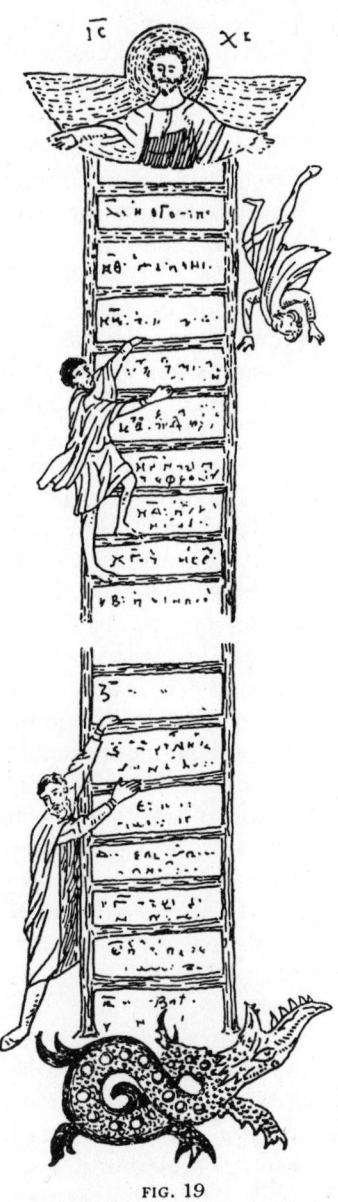

FIG. 19
Souls ascending, from a manuscript of the eleventh century (private collection)

These are not the only two stories; a hundred others bear witness to the same attitude. And of course it was to be expected; since the Empire recognized Christ as its master it had to admit that it was ruled by His will, the divine will. In her thinking, then, Byzantium soared above the principle of cause and effect and material laws. As she saw life, events did not follow one another according to strict logic but according to decisions made in heaven. The world she believed in was not like ours, a world of natural order, but a kaleidoscopic world constantly upset by divine intervention, where miracles became part of the daily routine.

This led to an everyday philosophy the exact opposite of that which most people in our time act upon. To have some part in shaping your own fate, do not bend and toil over this earth, but lift your gaze to the heavens. Up there and not down here will you find the solution of all troubles, the answer to all questions. If difficulty arises, pray. The best of clinics, indeed the only one, was the church. That is why Byzantium had so many of them; there were 67 dedicated to the Virgin alone, of which the most frequented was that of the Blachernae, famed for its Friday mystery.

The trance was the way to truth. The wise man was he who could achieve a state of ecstasy, for from that condition came the matrix which carried Christ's messages to earth. Laboratories and scientific apparatus were irrelevant. The Pasteurs of Byzantium walked about bare-footed and in rags, and their only equipment was inward vision. There were indeed several schools of knowledge; but they only differed as to the best means of achieving a state of grace. The monk's cell was one means, the hermit's cave another, but best of all was the pillar. 'Mount a column, never come down again and you will see how your perception will be sharpened.' Such was the claim of the Stylites who, practising what they preached, added a new picture to the album of human folly, already well stocked. Certain of them have left us the edifying example of their lives. Arsinos lived for 40 years on a pedestal near Damascus. St Alypios the Paphlagonian governed his monastery for 53 years from the top of a post and got down only when paralysed. In the fifth century there was Daniel of whom Theodosius II sent for news after each storm and whom he persuaded to build a little roof over his head. Eager as usual to enjoy the same advantages as men, the women of Byzantium defended their right to live such a gracious life and some of them became Stylites too.

FIG. 20
*Ascetics of the ninth century
(Firmin Didot Collection)*

In this society which disdained material laws the sciences remained embryonic, were restricted to the working out of recipes.

Arithmetic was in its infancy. There was no decimal system, there were no numbers: the letters of the alphabet were used for counting. Astronomy had not got beyond Ptolemy: the universe was a collection of revolving spheres with the earth at the centre. The only rival theory was that the earth is rectangular and flat-sided like a room, with the sky as ceiling. The sun was a little globe which disappeared at night behind a high conical mountain; the ocean surrounds us on all sides, hiding from us land inhabited by man before the Flood.

In the *Geoponics*, a treatise which was supposed to be more a treasure than a book, there is strange advice on agricultural matters. To prevent wine from turning sour it is sufficient to inscribe words from Psalm 34 on the barrels: 'O taste and see that the Lord is good!' To prevent getting drunk: eat the lung of a roasted goat, or bitter almonds or fully-grown cabbage; wear a crown of herb-ivy; best of all, while drinking the first cup say these words of Homer: 'But from the heights of Mount Ida the wise Jupiter flung down a thunderbolt upon them.' To rid the dovecote of serpents, write at each corner the word Αδαμ, which is composed of the initial letters of the cardinal points. For successful fishing you should thoroughly clean a shellfish, write certain magic words on its shell and throw it into the water. Fruit will not fall off a tree on which a verse of Homer is carved and similarly a verse from the first psalm will prevent it from rotting on the branches. To cure a sick donkey you need only tie round its neck a piece of papyrus bearing a certain long formula.

Medicine was a collection of old wives' tales. St Gregory's salt, made from ammonia, ginger, parsley, spikenard, siphium and pepper, would cure gout, cough, eye trouble, inadequacies of the spleen and baldness. Jamblic salt mixed with fish or meat stock or swallowed with a raw egg 'induces a gentle motion in the stomach', above all in those of 'a cold constitution'. To dispel headaches or improve eyesight, sauces should be seasoned with St Luke's salt, which is a mixture of aniseed, carrot, fennel, marjoram and roasted common salt. Drunken vapours are dissipated by King Ptolemy's remedy, Manethon's salt. Indigestion and 'sweating of the upper part of the body and the head' [*sic*] could be cured with Polles' salts, a compound of dry powdered camomile flowers, crushed fleabane, eryngium roots, marjoram and pepper.

What could be expected indeed of a therapy based on the belief that there were four humours in the body—blood, phlegm, yellow bile and black bile—and that good health depended upon their proper union with the four degrees: dry, humid, warm and cold!

Naturally Byzantium was unaware of the value of hygiene and

sanitation. The streets had a repulsive stench. Men and beasts sank into the excrement of camels, donkeys and horses, stepping upon rotten vegetables and slipping on the remains, tripping over fish refuse of all sorts that had been thrown out of houses and shops. Everybody who could went by horse, litter or carriage. This dirtiness was inexcusable, for there was water in abundance, even more than there was in Rome. It was brought down from the mountains in large quantities by many aqueducts, some of which were gigantic, like that built by Philoxenus for Constantine the Great, which, 65 feet high, was supported by 224 double columns and led the water into immense underground reservoirs. Though street lighting was poor—it was said to make more soot than light—it marked progress, for Rome had none, and when Caesar went abroad at night he was accompanied by two elephants bearing torches in their trunks.

Building followed no over-all plan of development, but houses were put up wherever it was possible. The huts of the poor stood side by side with the dwellings of the rich. The eye might pass straight from a miserable cabin to a marble palace of two stories, built in the Roman fashion with a plain façade and an interior court usually decorated by a fountain or some exotic curiosity. One of Zeno's laws tried timidly to impose a minimum width for the streets—usually 20 feet—and to fix a minimum distance between balconies. But ladies of leisure could always spy through their windows on to the daily lives of their neighbours.

To the lack of public hygiene there corresponded, of course, a malodorous unconcern for personal hygiene. A few sovereigns vainly conducted campaigns for personal cleanliness. Irene Ducas ordered that the pensioners in her convent should bathe once a month. One of the Comneni laid down two showers per week for the inmates of his hospital. But these were the exceptions. Reading the following sentence in the first treaty which the Byzantines made with Russian merchants one is tempted to smile at its hypocrisy: 'During their stay the Russians must take baths, which will be made available to them free of charge.' The men covered their filth under long garments of stiff brocade (inspired by the Huns), high, wide turbans, or pointed hats trimmed with fur, and large beards. The women applied several layers of make-up to their faces. History records the horrified

PLATE 6.
*San Vitale,
Ravenna*

*Church of the
Theotokos
Prinkipo*

PLATE 7.
Church of the Virgin Pammakaristos (11th century)

Church of St Irene (6th century)

Hagia Sophia as it was before the capture of Constantinople

amazement of the Burgundian La Broucquière on seeing the amount of make-up used by the Empress Irene, who was in fact one of the most beautiful women in the Empire.

In such a society, where so few calls were made on reason—that tool of a materialist world—the brain atrophies; in Byzantium the whole of intellectual life was stagnant. Literature was poverty stricken, living on what it had inherited from Greece and Rome. The most popular writings were chronicles of past times in which in a jumble of 'futility, idle talk and convent gossip'[1] the author usually limited himself to copying a predecessor. For a religious writer the highest achievement was reproduction of the thoughts of the Fathers with appropriate ecstatics. It was the boast of John the Damascene that there was nothing new in his work; a man like Origen was looked upon with disfavour as too inquiring. The Antioch school met with disapproval because it was too subtle. 'In history, theology and the sciences, what a lack of original work there is!' exclaims Rambaud. 'As regards Byzantine activity in philosophy the principal works are compilations. The greatest savant, Photius, is best known for his summary of ancient knowledge, the Myriobiblon.'[2]

The Byzantines had an excellent excuse ready for their mental laziness. They summarized the classics to make them easier to read, 'to provoke the more sustained attention of those who feed upon literature and impress more strongly on their minds those things that are worthy to be remembered'.

The schools produced not the full man, but the erudite. The pupil had to commit to memory a host of facts and dates, to learn Homer by heart and to stifle any personal opinion. This is what a test looked like:

Q. Who was the father of Hector?
A. Priam.
Q. Give the names of his brothers.
A. Alexander and Deiphobus.
Q. And his mother?
A. Hecuba.
Q. How do we know?
A. Through Homer, but Hellenicus and other writers have dealt with the subject.

---
[1] Diehl, *Byzance, Grandeur et Décadence*. [2] Rambaud, *L'Empire grec au 10e siècle*.

Distortion became so great, and routine and laziness so deeply rooted, that fidelity to what was old became a mania in Byzantium. When a new church was to be built it was not done with new materials. No, twenty monuments were pulled down to provide what was necessary. The statue of Anastasius was the demolished statue of Theodosius I. St Sophia was nothing but a vast assembly of marble columns and goldsmith's work from all the temples and churches of the Orient. 'It seemed as if medieval Greece could only get ideas and materials by stripping ancient Greece.'[1]

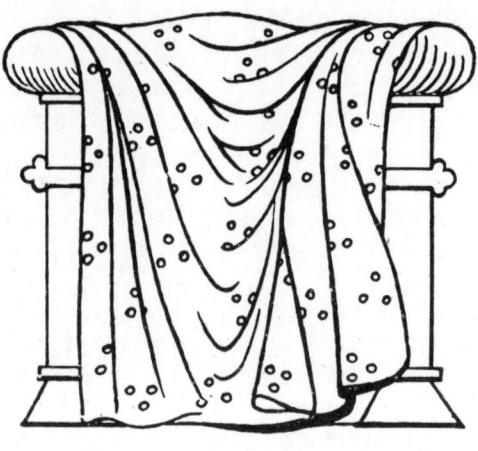

FIG. 21

Bisellium, or backless chair; the seat of honour in the municipia *(from a tenth century manuscript in the Beaunier and Rathier Collection)*

There was another consequence of this deprecation of reason, and it was not the least unusual one. Along with this rather more elevated form of mythomania, there was a degraded manifestation of it: the belief in fortune-telling, magic and sorcery. Byzantium was the homeland of palmists. Their headquarters were at the Hippodrome. These dealers in illusions set up shop under its arches, near the cages of the wild animals, not far from the icy water tanks and the medicinal baths, in the open air or in some obscure den. They were not content to sell love philtres to jealous women or pound the dung of the wild boar for a nervous charioteer. They did not hesitate to predict the most fantastic futures for their customers. On hearing that one day he would be a general, a patriarch, or even Basileus, some poor luckless creature who up to that time had had hardly a word to say for himself, would rush out to the public arena. There he would

[1] Rambaud, *L'Empire grec au 10e siècle.*

THE KINGDOM OF CHRIST ON EARTH

have no difficulty in finding credulous followers. Conspiracies and plots followed. Sometimes they succeeded.

If Leo III had not met two Jewish fortune tellers near a fountain one day, he would certainly never have become Basileus. The story is told that Bardanius the tutor of Michael the Stammerer was walking meditatively in the country, when a passing monk spoke to him. 'Stop thinking about the purple, you will never wear it. But these three'—and with his hand he indicated the three servants—'each one will be Emperor'. They were the men who became Leo V, Michael II and the usurper Thomas. For several nights a lunatic girl prevented the Basileus Michael Rangabé from sleeping. 'Go,' she cried, 'give your place to another. Soon you will be dethroned.' And before long her candidate, a stable boy, was crowned. Michael the Stammerer had no further doubt about his future when Leo V handed him his own garment and he accidentally trod on the edge of the Imperial mantle.

As for Basil I, what predictions he received! This giant shepherd, an Armenian by birth, 'half faun, half Antinous', after a long journey had just arrived in the capital to seek his fortune. Night had fallen and, tired and hungry, he settled down by the doorway of a monastery.

FIG. 22

Basil I, the giant shepherd, 'half faun, half Antinous' (from a manuscript)

During the night the holy martyr Diomedes appeared to the abbot of the monastery. 'Rise,' he said, 'and let the Emperor in.' His eyes swollen with sleep, the abbot stumbled to the door; he saw only a ragged peasant and, grumbling, returned to bed. A quarter of an hour later he was roused again, got up, went to the door, saw the peasant again and returned to bed. This time

Providence was angry and, we are assured, in order to clear his brain, poked the abbot in the ribs and said, 'He who sleeps outside is the Emperor.' Within an hour the bewildered countryman had been given a perfumed bath, an embroidered garment and was eating a sumptuous meal. Later he entered the service of the Peloponnesian commander. One morning he accompanied his master to the church at Patrae. Inside was a monk renowned for his laziness: he hardly ever got out of his chair. The provincial governor passed but he did not move. Yet when the humble servant approached, the man of God leapt to his feet and prostrated himself. Honours and wealth soon began to pour upon Basil. He was received at court and became in turn Chief Equerry and Grand Chamberlain. Knitting his brows, the First Minister, Caesar Bardas, commented, 'There is the lion which one day will devour us all'. Whereupon Theodora, the Emperor's mother, who was a student of the occult, fainted in terror.

One must realize how such predictions were taken seriously by third parties. No sooner had the verminous monk mentioned the royal purple, than Leo the stable boy was urged by a general to marry his daughter. Basil the servant was carried off by a rich widow. The obscure Marcianus received as a present the considerable sum of two hundred nomismata. The effect of the predictions on those involved could be terrifying.

Faced by such dangers, a number of emperors took rigorous measures. None were completely successful, for it was difficult to prevent mysticism from degenerating among the people into superstition. The step from a prayer to an incantation, from a priest to a magician is often short, and Byzantium, the city of Christ, was the city of collective delusion. It was said that there were mystic writings on certain columns that indicated the names of future Emperors, the date of the destruction of the capital, the tears shed by the last Basileus before going into exile. (A strange point, this: the Byzantines knew their Empire to be condemned.) By unscrewing the hoof of a brass horse which stood in one of the public squares, one could find the name of the barbarian who would overthrow the monarchy. The spirit of Justinian wandered through the Sacred Palace at night with its head in its hands. Satan appeared to Bishop Parthenius of Lampsacus in the form of a fierce dog. Alexander had parti-

THE KINGDOM OF CHRIST ON EARTH

cular care taken of a bronze lion in the Circus, for he was certain that he would perish if any accident befell it. It was by decapitating a particular statue in the Xerolophon that Byzantium brought about the death of the great Bulgarian Tsar Simeon, etc.

This passion for the supernatural and scorn for the worldly can today surprise or amuse us. But in its own epoch it corresponded to a fundamental need. The outside world was hard,

FIG. 23

Ascension of Alexander, after a bas-relief at St Mark's, Venice

full of pain, fear and uncertainty. Century after century the barbarians snarled beyond the frontiers. Often they broke the dikes and spread over the provinces or the sea. Sometimes their armies had reached the very walls of the capital. Huns, Persians, Bulgarians, Saracens and Russians had all tried to take the town. Because dangers constantly threatened, every citizen must keep three months' provisions in his home. The simple happiness and laughter of the pagan were lost. Reassurance must be sought in the beyond, a god was needed to still one's inquietude, the thought of eternal life made present sufferings bearable. For sovereign one must have the Son of the All Powerful.

APPENDIX

The Bogomile Heresy

The Bogomile religion, the source of the Albigensian heresy, came from Bulgaria. Its adherents went out into the world to preach revolt in the name of the Lord. Their message was, on the face of it, rather a joyful one: there shall be no more authority and no more discipline. The vassal was to be released from his oath, the subject from his duty of obedience, the taxpayer from taxation and the convict from his punishment. Nothing belonged to Caesar. Authority is a creation of the devil. Everything is permissible here below, theft included. Only personal authority and superiority and their manifestations are the work of the devil.

What need was there for armies and wars, which destroyed the body, but did not purify the soul? The Bogomile was anti-militarist. What need was there for churches, if God was everywhere? The Bogomile was anti-clerical. What need was there for the State, if independent communities could bring back the equality of the early Christians? He was an anarchist.

These beliefs did not prevent the Bogomiles from living in hierarchical communities. At the top were the Fathers who, assisted by two vicars, their 'sons' and successors, 'the elder deacon' and 'the junior deacon', administered wide areas, just as bishops do. At an intermediate level were the Perfect Ones, whose attributes were predominantly spiritual. They recited the Lord's Prayer, the only permitted one, blessed the bread without, however, making the sign of the cross; and by folding their hands prevented the dying man from either being damned or being reborn in the form of an ox. As a sign of gratitude, the dying man who recovered must live an exemplary life; any departure from the straight and narrow path and he must take a drink containing crushed glass, or receive a dagger in the heart or have his veins severed.

Fathers and Perfect Ones did not lead enviable lives. They must not eat meat, cheese, eggs, butter, milk or oil—the foods of Satan; they had to break completely with the outside world; flee from gatherings, marriages, popular celebrations and taverns; leave wives and children; speak as little as possible; take no part in legal proceedings; were not to go to war, kill, defend their own lives or resist evil; and if their salvation demanded it, they had to let themselves die of hunger or be suffocated with a pillow. On the other hand, they were entitled to an outward show of respect: in approaching them one bent the knee and touched the ground three times with one's forehead.

The entire Bogomile philosophy was based on the belief, so popular amongst the Slavs, in two Gods constantly at war with one another: the White God, who was the source of good, and the Black God, the source of evil. They made changes to the Book of Genesis in a way that increased the role of the devil and gave him divine stature. According to this, the earth was not created by God, but by his eldest son, Satanael, who was angered by his fall. Adam too was his creation, but as he was imperfect from the start (for soul he had only a kind of liquid humour, a drop of which escaped from his foot and made the serpent). Satanael proposed a sort of gentlemen's agreement to God, his father. If God would take Adam over to perfect him he could have a half share in him. God agreed and our ancestor lived thus for some time in the service of two masters. But joint ownership is often a source of disagreement, and it was not long before Satanael broke the agreement. He seduced Eve and gave her two children, a son called Cain and a daughter Kalomene, that is, Perfection. His partner took the affair badly and meted out a rigorous penalty; he took away his beauty and his creative power. Then everything went from bad to worse. As though illustrating a theory dear to Francis de Croisset, when he became ugly and dirty, Satanael became wicked. He did to us what God had done to him. He turned the faithful from the narrow path, he inspired the murder of Abel and seduced the fallen angels with girls. He brought on the Flood and saved only his devoted servant Noah. He it was who confounded the tongues of men and scattered them to the four corners of the earth. He destroyed Sodom and Gomorrha. It was he who, supreme wickedness—the Bogomile was anti-semitic—appeared one day on Sinai and put Moses on earth 'with his wicked commandments' and the prophets 'with their wicked advice'. Finally, after nearly 5,500 years, God showed some concern. From his heart sprang another son, Michael, the future Jesus. But he must appear in flesh and blood; the change was effected through Mary's ears. Entering her right ear as a free spirit, the Messiah emerged from her left ear clothed in flesh and blood. Nothing could have been more chaste; we may note, incidentally, that the Bogomiles regarded marriage with horror. Satanael heard what had happened and lay in wait for his brother, determined to get rid of him. It was Satanael who arranged Christ's crucifixion, but happily Christ came to life again and Satanael was punished: he was turned into Satan and relegated to hell. But this fall did not finally settle the problem; the recurrence of similar calamities must be avoided. So God brought forth another son, the Holy Spirit, whose task it was to help souls to purify themselves. However, Jesus did not succeed in securing from his father the neutralization of the devils and they continue to haunt reliquaries, icons, temples, the liturgy and the sacraments, and to play a thousand tricks on us—the worst being the miracles. Thus, in spite of exorcisms and propitiatory sacrifices, many years will pass before the universal deliverance and the return of the world to happy anarchy.[1]

The Bogomiles were always friendly and eager and made many converts. 'Like sheep, they had gentle and peaceful faces, they were quiet, and pale with fasting,' wrote Cosmas. 'Their approach was modest and they simply said that they sought a path to Heaven.' They benefited also from the surrounding misery and the unworthiness of the ruling classes. Above all, they could speak to their listeners in terms that could be understood; they always had fables and thrilling stories to tell. In their hands the Gospel became a saga of astrology and prophecy. Every important person in the New Testament[2] was made the hero of a highly coloured epic full of imaginary exploits. Told in great detail, these tales kept their listeners breathless. There were 'The Travels in Hell of the Mother of God', 'The Legend of the Cross', 'The Testament and the Twelve Patriarchs', 'The Trials of Isaiah' and many others.

The most unlikely subjects did not discourage them. Thus the High Priest Jeremy devoted a most edifying tract to St Vitus' dance and kindred complaints.[3]

---

[1] The Bogomiles did not recognize images, use temples or observe the feasts of the calendar. They mocked marriage and miracles and prayed in the open air or in their homes.

[2] The Old Testament was for them a creation of the devil.

[3] Here is a simple extract:
'Near the Red Sea stood a stone column on which the Holy Apostle Sisinnus was sitting looking at the sea. Suddenly there came a wave as high as the sky and out of it stepped twelve women with long hair. They said "We are Herod's daughters". "Accursed demons, why have you come here?" demanded St Sisinnus. "We have come to torment the human race. We shall pounce on him who gets drunk and torment him; he who sleeps on duty, who does not pray to God, who drinks and eats as soon as he rises—they are all ours."
'St Sisinnus prayed to God, saying, "Lord, save mankind from these accursed demons." And Christ sent him two angels, called Sichael and Anos, as well as the four evangelists, who began to beat the daughters of Herod with an iron rod, giving them three thousand strokes every day. They begged for mercy, saying, "Do not beat us, only tell us your holy names and we shall go far away." St Sisinnus asked them, "What are *your* names?" The first one said, "The Trembler". The

They had an explanation for everything. The moon was pale because it had sinned; while the sun, the stars and the angels had shed tears over the nudity of Adam and Eve after the first sin, alone in the universe, it had refused to weep; so God punished it by dimming its light. Herod's twelve daughters bring fever to us. But to say the name of St Sisinnus, or better still, to recite his prayer of exorcism, is enough to make those female devils flee, and so be cured.

The writer Bogoslav offered a thousand and one revelations of the secrets of Heaven, the Creation and the last judgment. The Antichrist will have hair stiff and sharp like arrows, his eyes will shine like the Morning Star, his fingers will be as sharp as billhooks. After his defeat the dead will come to life, the world will catch fire, and a hurricane of wind and dust will make it as white and flat as a sheet of parchment, without the smallest valley or mountain.

How many listeners must have felt dizzy on hearing, for example, the following description of the foundations of our planet! It floats on a limitless ocean which rests upon a rocky plain; this plain rests upon four peaks which are supported on a river of fire. The river rests upon an iron oak tree whose roots plunge into the power of God, and so on.

The Slav people readily took all this in. To some extent, it echoed their ancient superstitions, their more recent polytheism, and for a long time the heresy was widely accepted; it is, however, much more surprising to find it so vigorous in Western Europe in the eleventh and twelfth centuries.

second said "Burning Fever"; for just as the fire in the stove burns pitchy wood, so the great fever burns the body of a man. The third said, "Frost"; for she makes a man's body tremble as in great cold and he cannot get warm even inside the stove. The fourth said, "I am called Oppression"; she weighs upon a man's side so that he can no longer eat. The fifth said, "I am called Ginusa"; she weighs upon a man's head and breaks his shoulders so that he coughs. The sixth said, "I am Deafness"; she falls upon a man's head and blocks up his ears and breaks his head. The seventh said, "I am called the Breaker"; she breaks a man's skull and bones as a great wind breaks rotten wood. The eighth said, "I am the Blower"; when she blows she makes tempers to rise. The ninth said, "I am called Jaundice"; she is the colour of a yellow flower in the fields. The tenth said, "I am the Render"; she is the worst of all, for she tears the veins of the hands and feet. The eleventh said, "I am called Glodoja"; she too is worst of all, for in the night she will not let a man sleep, so that the demons swoop down on him and his reason wanders. The twelfth said, "I am Novoja"; she is the oldest of us all. It was she who cut off St John's head, and when she takes possession of a man, he must die.'

II

SOCIAL STRIFE
AND
ECONOMIC
STABILITY

A Strange Class War

It is one thing to set up godly institutions and another to live up to them. In Byzantium the Gospel shaped the constitution but it certainly did not shape men's hearts. In this most Christian Empire the most treacherous, savage, implacable class-war raged. Nothing tempered it; nothing justified it. It was not waged, as in our time, for an ideal of social justice; no technical arguments, no economic theories were set forth to support it. The situation was simple, crude and the reverse of the one we know. Here it was the wealthy and the powerful who ceaselessly attacked the weak as though they would devour them entirely. The background was not of grey factory chimneys, but the smiling pastures of the countryside. The victim, the prey, was the small farmer; the aggressor the great rural landlord.

Rarely had there been such a combination of circumstances for the temptation and torment of fallible man: on the one hand completely unsheltered weakness; on the other an excess of power. The small man, constantly the victim of war, pillage, taxation and poor harvests, was always on the brink of want. The strong, on the other hand, not only possessed economic wealth, but were the highest public officials in the district, for in Byzantium the possession of a vast estate conferred the right to high administrative office, while, conversely, promotion to high rank in government was accompanied by an endowment of land. Could the wealthy have resisted temptation? And how could the weak resist their attacks? Thus the Byzantine countryside was the scene of a play with a tragic theme but many comic situations.

Sometimes a great landowner (*dunatos*) would seek out a peasant (*penes*) and speak to him somewhat as follows. 'Greetings, my friend. You know, I've never understood why you go on struggling like this against the weather, tax collectors and bandits, when a comfortable living is within your grasp! All you have to do is accept me as a tenant. I will pay a substantial rent,

FIG. 24
*Mosaic in the Great Mosque of Damascus
Painted over by the Turks and uncovered about 1935*

you know.' The peasant thinks that he has not understood; was he, the disinherited, to have the great landlord as tenant? 'Yes, of course!' The peasant's heart beats with pride and his purse already feels heavier on his belt—he is not familiar with Virgil's *Timeo Danaos* . . .! He falls to his knees and kisses his benefactor's robe. But when the rich man has entered into the tenancy he does not pay any rent. Before the court he is haughty and rather amused. What nonsense! That he should be the tenant of a serf! He is using this land because he is indeed its proprietor. By these methods, and perhaps by a bribe to the judge beforehand, he wins his case. Not only has he got away without paying a penny, but henceforth the land is his.

In years of bad harvest—which, alas! were frequent—the *humilior* faced bankruptcy. Taxes were heavy. Then the *potentior* sent one of his agents to the village, who, assuming a disinterested manner, advised the poor man to sell his holding. He happened to know a buyer and offered to speak to him. Before long the peasant had parted with his land for a mouthful of bread.

Occasionally there was a scene which was pure farce, like the following. A childless peasant is dying. The landowner quickly despatches a messenger to his bedside. 'You know, for a long time my master has respected you and admired you. He wants to know how you are and whether there is anything he can send you.' A few presents add to the effect. Soon the sick man, burning with pride and fever, is in the right mood; he would like to make some gesture in return. 'Nothing could be simpler,' the messenger declares. 'Be so good as to adopt my master!' Dizzy with pride and weakened by suffering, the old man agrees. A priest is hurriedly called from a nearby chapel and he, well-versed in the business, gives it his solemn blessing. All that one has to do now is await the end, and that can be speeded up if necessary.

Sometimes the *dunatos* were more treacherous. They deliberately created a thousand troubles and vexations for the *penes*. Naturally, they hid behind a man-of-straw: for example, the tax collector would be bribed suddenly to increase his demands, or a brigand would be paid to ravage the district. Then in the village the poor peasant talked to everyone about his misfortunes.

As though by chance, some servant of his real tormentor was there and joined in the conversation, offering advice. 'Why do you complain, when the lord is so good and so well-disposed to the weak? Without a doubt, he will give you his protection. I'll speak to him about it if you like.' Taken aback, the poor dupe kissed the man's hands and the very next day received a wonderful offer: until the trouble was over his property could be put under the cover of the great man's name. Unsuspectingly he signed an agreement provisionally making over his possessions. He never saw them again.

To make a will in Byzantium one needed only to bring three witnesses together. Thus, when a peasant was near to death, his humble home often became the scene of strange happenings: from morning to night the agents of the *dunatos* besieged him. When he finally expired they ran quickly to a magistrate to swear that the deceased had bequeathed all the disposable portion of his estate—perhaps two-thirds of his goods—to their master.

When the *humilior* needed money—and that was frequently the case—the *potentior* sent a servant to make the offer of a loan. The rate of interest was high but the poor man had no choice, so he agreed. The very first time that he failed to pay, the creditor took possession. A variation on this manoeuvre was to secure the receipt before handing over the loan. Then the *potentior* 'forgot' to pay but he did not forget to put a distraint upon the peasant the first time payment was due, as indicated on the receipt.

Although such proceedings abused the faith of the peasants and in the long run defeated themselves, there was another which was more open and even more formidable: the *patrocinium*. Tired at last of a profitless liberty in which trouble and poverty were his only companions, the *penes* agreed to surrender ownership of his property to the *dunatos*, reserving to himself the usufruct only. Protected by the great man's name, he no longer feared tax gatherers, magistrates, robbers or other powerful people. As the lord wanted to encourage such practices, the peasant sometimes even received the produce of some of his farms. His situation was thus improved. But on his death his goods did not pass on to his family who fell into the ranks of the landless.

The most insatiable in this rural scramble were the monks. Gone were the days when their virtue was an example to Egypt, Palestine and Alexandria. No longer was this earth a bitter road to eternity, but a place of delights where they did not scorn to gorge themselves. A fig for self-mastery! Long live my neighbour's riches! Acre by acre they absorbed the estates, and head by head the flocks and herds. Horses, cattle, sheep and camels, all were most welcome. The preachers of poverty, austere and inspired, had become fat and jolly landed proprietors. They no longer left it to God to feed them as He feeds the little birds, but they gave full rein to their greed, astuteness and gluttony. And often it seemed all too easy, for in this devout empire it was the custom to give generously to the church. Moreover it was the church and not the State which administered the various charitable institutions—orphanages, homes for incurables, hostels for travellers. And what endowments they received!

It is understandable that there were swarms of monks. How could the obscure peasant from Thrace, or some other province, who was plagued daily by hunger, pillage and conscription resist the call of the religious orders with their promise of abundance, security and universal respect? Gradually the monasteries emptied the Empire of men and goods.[1]

There were consequences which the authorities could not contemplate with indifference. A feudal society was emerging in which the general interest was put second to those of the landed proprietors. The middle class was slowly disappearing and with its proletarization the threat of social strife was growing. Receipts from taxation were falling, for the peasant proprietor had been the chief source of revenue; the big men, legally or otherwise, escaped taxation.

Imperial security was threatened. When the connection with the soil was broken national pride and patriotic devotion began to wither. A man had no ardour in defending a State which allowed him to be despoiled. This danger was most obvious when the *dunatoï* began to attack the military fiefs that were given to soldiers to make it possible for them to live and equip themselves.

[1] Ferradou noted that when the Turks took Constantinople, a third of the land of the Empire belonged to the monasteries. (Ferradou, *Des biens des monastères à Byzance*.)

So the emperors adopted a series of measures: forbidding the landlords to take over the debts of the *penes*, and the *penes* to hand over his possessions to the *dunatos*. This was what was called the prohibition of affixing *tituli* (it had been the custom for a threatened peasant to fasten on his doorway for protection a tablet bearing the name and arms of a powerful lord, this simple act being enough to secure transfer of ownership). In the case of a loan the burden of proof was transferred, a seller was permitted to cancel a sale and a tenant an agreement which turned out to be unfair, and anyone could withdraw from a contract before it had been put into effect.

Most comprehensive of all, three complementary novellae of the tenth century made it illegal for the *potentior* to receive from the *humilior* any advantage from adoption, gift, legacy, usufruct or *patrocinium*, and prohibited all sale or exchange between them and made prescription inoperable between them as a method of acquiring property.

When this stage was reached the two classes had ceased to exist legally for one another. What more could the government have done? And yet the *dunatoï* never did cease to expropriate, sapping to the very end the Empire's will to resist.

A Paradise of Privilege and Monopoly

It is easy to think of Byzantium as a languid city, basking under the blazing Eastern sun. At best she is credited with rather derisive activities, as evinced by the popularity of the fable that she continued to debate the sex of the angels while the Turks were scaling her ramparts.

But in the later Middle Ages not even Venice was more industrious. She might have parodied Plato's famous formula and proclaimed on her gates: 'Let no idle man enter here.'

In the first place, she tolerated no unemployed within her gates; to lose one's job was to be expelled. Then she made her most beautiful avenue, the Mese, into the business centre. To

SOCIAL STRIFE AND ECONOMIC STABILITY 87

appreciate the full significance of such an event we must imagine the Champs Elysées or Regent Street transformed into a noisy fair. For in Byzantium negotiations did not take place inside severely functional offices, but in the open air, in the middle of a seething, jostling crowd. There were no shops, but the tradesmen set out their wares by the roadside or on a bench in a booth. A customer would never have dreamt of going into a shop; what should he do in such a dark place? The counter-bench was the inviolate frontier from opposing sides of which

FIG. 25

(Left) Fifth century enamelled vase in blue shot with purple-brown
(Right) Green enamel vase of the fifth century
(from the former collection of Dr Fouquet of Cairo)

buyer and seller discussed and haggled to their hearts' content. Foodstuffs were not set out on the bench but remained in sacks and barrels—opened for display—so that the trader looked like a soldier entrenched behind sandbags.

It is difficult to describe the picturesqueness of these innumerable bazaars, animated and shining with a thousand colours, disgorging sumptuous cloths, embroidery with delicate gold patterns, marvellous goldsmiths' work, sparkling jewels, and finely sculptured ivory: full of the noise of bargaining, the bleating of sheep, whinnying of horses and grunting of pigs. Near St Sophia were the makers of wax tapers. The dealers in imported Syrian goods clustered near the Porticos. In turn the Strategion (until the first day of Lent) and the Forum Tauri (from Easter to Pentecost) were white with sheep. Near the Great Palace were the silversmiths, and even on the Augusteon the makers of perfume, an honour granted 'in order that the good odour of their wares might rise like incense towards the image of Christ which dominates the principal entry to the Imperial Residence'.

FIG. 26

Blue enamelled vase (former Fouquet Collection)

Seeing this seething, noisy, disorderly mass of men, animals and materials, one might think that the economic life of the Empire proceeded in an easy liberalism, free from all restraints and controls. The truth was quite otherwise. There was no economic freedom in Byzantium, everything was regulated. Here the true socialist city was in being long before Karl Marx and Lenin.

There were two reasons for this, the one moral, the other political. First, the church disapproved of free competition, looking upon it as a fratricidal struggle. Then, the government was always anxious about the provisioning of its capital. Thus everything and everybody in the Empire was submitted to a merciless discipline, the better to fill the stomachs and preserve the souls of these too revolutionary Christians. Byzantium has been well described as 'the paradise of privilege, monopoly and protection'. There can have been few communities whose economic life was as closely controlled as that of the Eastern Roman Empire.

The manufacturer who wanted to lay in a stock had to get in touch with a specified supplier: the baker with a government officer, the spinner with a named importer, the weaver with the State dye-works, the silk merchant with the weaver, etc. Either he was told how much to take or he was given a limit; the goldsmith might hold at any time not more than a pound of unminted gold. The horse dealers had to take the rejects brought to town by the peasants. The cloth merchants had to buy the whole import of fabrics from Syria. The fish merchants had to buy the whole catch. Certain things did not enter the market, such as yellow soap, then called 'Gaul Soap', which was strictly reserved for the use of the Emperor.

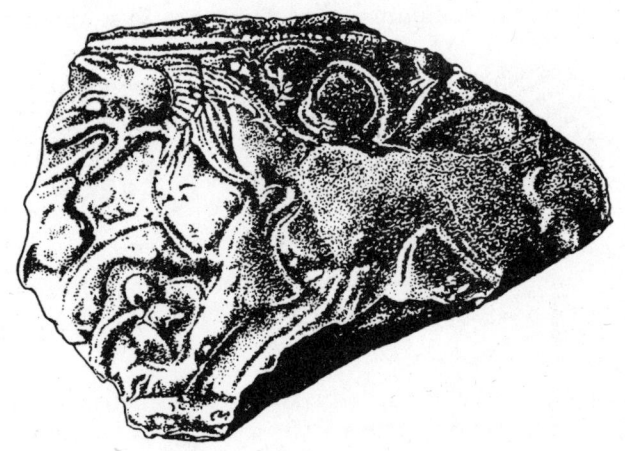

FIG. 27

Fragment of sixth century pottery (former Fouquet Collection)

Manufacturing was supervised by the State. The soapmaker was told what materials to use. The candle maker must not use inferior wax or oil remainder or animal fat. The weaver must avoid certain purples known as 'prohibited' and the object of a State monopoly, and had to observe surprisingly detailed regulations.

Selling was the subject of a whole series of controls. Often a man could not choose his own customer: the silk importer must deal with the spinner, the spinner with the State dye-works, the State dye-works with the weaver, the weaver with the seller of silk goods, and so on.

Stock-piling of consumers' goods was not allowed. The scent maker could not store spices against a scarcity, the draper and the pig dealer could not withhold their goods in the hope of better prices.

The export of certain articles was forbidden; salted fish, raw silk and certain cloths were examples. So it was that the Jews, who were not trusted, could not deal in them. From this arose too the pitiless control to which foreign merchants were submitted in the capital; they were only tolerated for a limited time, usually three months; they were put in a specific resi-

FIG. 28

Coiffures (from various MSS and paintings)

dence, always outside the city walls, and their names were registered. They could expect visits from the police at any hour of the day and they had to be able to explain and justify what they were doing. When they visited the town they were accompanied by an official who carefully supervised their purchases. They could buy only certain specified goods and for greater security their resources were controlled. Severe conditions were imposed on them as sellers. If a foreign merchant tried to break any of the rules he was immediately stripped, shaven, whipped and ignominiously driven out. Even Russian merchants, who had the benefit of three commercial treaties dated 907, 911 and 944, could not come and go as they pleased. They had to carry a writ from the *Kniaz*, or Prince of Kiev, bearing their name, that of their ship and the nature of their business. Without special permission they were not allowed to buy silken goods above a certain value. Invariably they had to leave at the approach of winter. Only those who brought raw silk could be sure of a friendly reception. 'They,' said the edict, 'need not have a licence to sell and at a hostel they will only pay for the number of days they stay there.'

SOCIAL STRIFE AND ECONOMIC STABILITY

A man could not set up shop just where he chose; the urban prefect allocated each place. He tried to group together all those engaged in the same trade, a cherished medieval custom. 'Only grocers may have a shop anywhere in the town.'

The shop itself could not necessarily embody its owner's ideas. There had to be, for instance, a gap of 70 yards between shops selling wax and candles. Size was the subject of regulation and no shop was to be so big that it could hold more than ten people. Bankers, silversmiths and goldsmiths had to provide themselves with a permanent armed guard, they had to prevent loitering near their premises, were to have piles of money always available on their counters, and might not leave their shops for any reason whatsoever. Their employees could not be permitted to deal alone with a customer, nor be sent through the streets with money. Bakers were not allowed to set themselves up under a dwelling house for, as the edict explained, 'inflammable materials warm the ovens'.

FIG. 29

Silk fabric (in the Museum of Industrial Art, Crefeld)

Certain people were not even allowed to have a shop. The linen weaver had, like a hawker or old-clothes dealer, to tour the town with his goods on his shoulder; no one knew why. The importer of raw silk had to display all his goods on the public highway in full daylight, in this case to avoid any black market dealings.

It was prohibited to set up shops with many products. Each

FIG. 30

A mosaic at Tyre (from Didron's 'Annales Archéologiques')

man must have his own speciality. Goldsmiths were limited to work in gold, silver and precious stones; bankers to exchanging and lending money; linen drapers to the purchase and manufacture of linen. Makers of scent were restricted to trade in spices—pepper from the Indies, spikenard from Laodicia, cinnamon from Asia and Ceylon, aloes from China, Java or Sumatra, musk from Tibet, incense, myrrh and balsam from Arabia, 'sweet-smelling beet', *lazouray* (which was sometimes used as a purgative and sometimes as seasoning) and above all ambergris from the East. Candle makers were allowed to deal only in candles and soap makers only in soap. Harness makers could only work in leather. Butchers were limited to the purchase and slaughter of animals and the retail trade in meat, fishmongers to the sale of fresh fish, bakers to the grinding of corn and sale of bread, café owners to the provision of food and drink. Grocers could sell meat, salted fish, which was highly prized, flour, cheese, honey, olive oil, various vegetables, butter, resin, tar, cedar oil, hemp, oakum, gypsum, crockery (it was usually earthenware), bottles and nails.

Specialization was pushed to extreme lengths in the case of silk. First quality raw silk might be bought and sold only by *metaxoprates*, second quality by *metathrarioi*. First preparation was exclusively the work of *katartaires* and dyeing that of the State workshops. The manufacture of silken goods was the speciality and monopoly of the *serikaires* and their sale was the work of *vestioprates*. The buying and selling of the various stuffs imported from Syria was the absolute monopoly of the *prandioprates*.

It was forbidden to form a trust or cartel or even to open a branch shop. The law disapproved of any attempt to corner the market and its officers would proceed against anyone 'who tries to increase the number of his shops so that everybody would have to deal with him'.

One was not permitted to fix one's own prices, but had to conform to the prefect's tariff, which varied according to the known supply. For this reason the fishmongers had to seek him out every morning to tell him how much tunny had been caught during the night. Butchers and innkeepers must inform him each time they took a delivery. The edict also said, 'Bakers will visit the prefect each time there is a rise in the price of wheat so that the weight of loaves may be adjusted'.

Everyone's profit was strictly limited; that of grocers, for example, to fifteen per cent of the selling price. Every fortune was suspect, and the newly-rich risked having his goods confiscated, like Philocale.

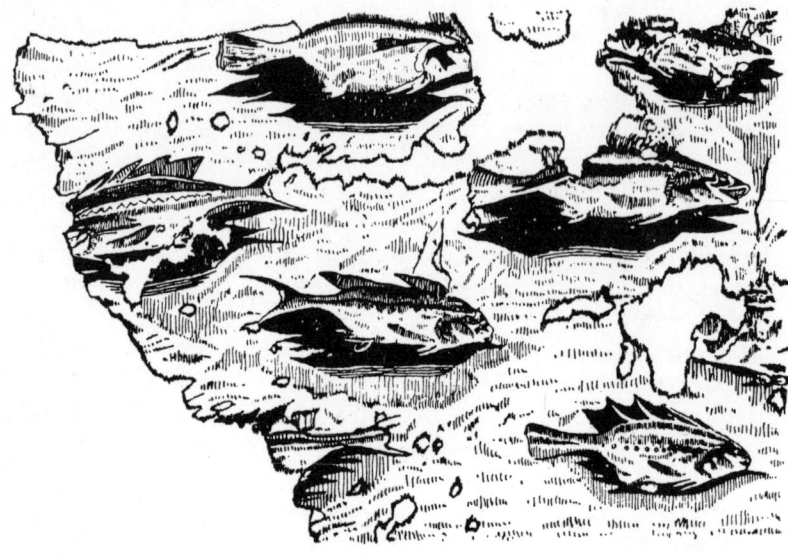

FIG. 31
Hellenistic tapestry of the third to fourth centuries (at Lyons)

Only stamped weights and measures might be used and the candle maker's scales and the cups in the café were marked with the prefect's seal.

Work on certain days, or even at certain times, was forbidden. Novella 54 of the Emperor Leo stated: 'All work is forbidden on Sundays and feast days so that people occupied in commerce and industry may attend public worship and follow the ceremonies.'

Only grocers, candle makers and cafés were exempt from this regulation, but they were not allowed to open before a stated time, generally eight o'clock in the morning. Cafés had to close each day at eight o'clock in the evening 'in order to avoid disturbance of the peace'.

SOCIAL STRIFE AND ECONOMIC STABILITY

Controls in Byzantium extended even over the relations between capital and labour. Wages were not fixed by bargaining but by the decision of the prefect. In connection with certain guilds, like that of the *serikaires* (the silk manufacturers), a form of collective contract forbade the hiring of workers for more than a month at a time.

Relations between artisans and clients were regulated in still greater detail. Thus the former might not go on strike except where the latter had failed either to provide the necessary materials or to make the required cash deposit. Prices were fixed by the job and could be changed only if considered grossly inadequate by the prefect. Qualified men must be employed for all important and delicate work. Finally, the architect's responsibility for solidity of construction extended over six years in most cases and over ten years in the case of freestone buildings. The Byzantine preoccupation with division of labour had the curious consequence that no single individual might be entrusted with the complete carrying out of a large project, such as the building of a house or palace. Painter, mason, etc., had to be approached separately, with the result that instead of just one contractor responsible for the whole job, there were several, each responsible for a part of it: one for the walls, one

FIG. 32

Bronze door at Salerno (made in Constantinople about 1085 for Robert Guiscard) for the arches, another for the domes, someone else for the balconies, and so on.

All these regulations naturally necessitated an elaborate system of control and supervision.

The first stage was connected with preventive measures: entry to a trade or profession was made dependent on presentation by sponsors, usually five, on the payment of a high fee—six or even ten besants—and on the approval of the prefect.

Then came measures of self-discipline: producers were gathered into guilds, which supervised their activities through a president nominated by the government.

At a third stage there was direct governmental control through a corps of labour inspectors, the *logothetes*, who were liable to enter a shop or workshop at any hour of the day or night.

Finally, the people were expected to co-operate; informing was a national custom and the number of anonymous letters was limited only by the extent of literacy.

Even the lightest punishment was severe and the urban prefect was pitiless. The goldsmith who had taken delivery of more than the permitted pound of unminted gold was fined the equivalent of £360. The candle maker who demanded a price higher than that stipulated by long-term contract was fined £220, as was the soap maker whose scales were inaccurate. The grocer guilty of deceit or of charging more than the official price was fined £55. Damages, in addition to fines, had to be paid; their amount was not dependent upon an estimate of compensation for the injury received, but upon the false price quoted. Thus a goldsmith guilty of fraud must pay to the seller the exact amount of the unfair appraisal he had made.

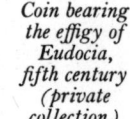

FIG. 33

Coin bearing the effigy of Eudocia, fifth century (private collection)

Serious misdeeds were punished by confiscation of all goods, including slaves.[1] 'Every goldsmith,' said the edict, 'who sells

---

[1] In spite of the efforts of the Church there was still slavery in Christian Byzantium. Many of the slaves were Saracen prisoners whose ransom had not been paid. Others were hungry looking creatures sold by their families or even by themselves.

SOCIAL STRIFE AND ECONOMIC STABILITY

a sacred object, complete or in part, without declaring the sale to the prefect, will be liable to the penalty of confiscation. The buyer will be liable to the same penalty.'

Expulsion from the craft or guild could be inflicted in certain cases: upon the goldsmith who failed to consult the prefect in fixing prices, or who merely quarrelled with his colleagues, upon the draper who put up the rent of a workshop in the hope of being able to take it over himself, the soap maker who used animal fat during Lent or on fast days, the grocer who sold above the fixed price. Banishment was the penalty for other offences: for the perfume maker who dealt in proscribed materials or set himself up in the wrong place, for example, for the butcher who built up stocks for the purpose of speculation.

Naturally, to these pecuniary punishments, corporal punishment was added. Flogging was the commonest. The guilty man was taken to the public square, tied to a post and before the populace received the prescribed number of lashes. Then his head was shorn so that for many weeks to come he would be conspicuous in a town like Constantinople where the hair was worn long. Or he might simply be paraded through the streets, sitting back to front on a donkey or a camel, the target for the taunts and jeers of the crowd. The sentence meted out to those who mishandled valuable objects was often the cutting off of a hand. 'Every goldsmith or banker who buys unminted gold for his own use shall have a hand cut off', said the edict.

FIG. 34

Golden coin bearing the effigy of Justinian II (private collection)

Sometimes the punishment was death—for using a poisonous substance in making soap, for example.

With this mass of rules and penalties one might have expected the Byzantine economy to be stifled; but far from being a hindrance, these regulations turned out to be a valuable asset. Firstly, over-production was avoided. Supply could readily be adapted to the generally known demand, and the prohibition of stock-piling ensured a smooth flow of economic life. Thus Byzantium never experienced industrial or commercial crises.

Again, importers purchased as a group: the foreign merchant found that he faced a united front and often had to lower his demands considerably. In co-operation with the prefect the association placed its order and divided up the purchase in accordance with members' requirements.

Insistence upon specialization must have resulted in a higher standard of craftsmanship, while making the growth of large monopolistic units impossible. Close supervision made for complete secrecy in manufacturing processes and thus helped Byzantium to dominate the world market for certain goods. Middlemen were eliminated. Producers dealt directly with one another and consumers dealt directly with producers. 'Thus,' said the edict in relation to *prandioprates*, 'whatever the nature of a consignment of Syrian goods, the association of *prandioprates* will buy all the clothing, both of superior and inferior quality. If there are perfumes or dyes, they will all be bought by the scent makers. If a noble or, in general, a citizen of the town wishes to buy a part of the consignment, he will be allowed to buy an amount which he can use in his own home.'

Finally the State was able to charge certain professions with official tasks and thus obtain free services. Bankers had to check the value of coins in circulation and to withdraw bad ones; they had the responsibility of tracking down the counterfeiters, the *sakkoularii*—so called from the name of the money-bag used on market days. Horse dealers had to examine each animal offered for sale on the market and point out its weaknesses to the purchaser. It was the duty of the *vestioprates*, successors of the Roman *vestiarii*, to decorate the town on the occasion of an official ceremony and in preparation for the triumphal entry of an emperor.

Byzantium's prosperity, however, was due not to regulation alone, but as much, if not more, to her geographical situation, her financial system and the skill of her citizens.

The town was situated on the main trade route between East and West, the route favoured by the great galleons and light feluccas sailing from India, Ceylon and China or from the western ports of Venice, Amalfi, Genoa and Marseilles. Often, successful wars tightened even more the control over commerce which Byzantium enjoyed. For instance, by seizing every point of access to the Black Sea, she managed to take over all the seaborne trade of South Russia. Riches from all corners of the earth found their way into the Byzantine warehouses.

From India came spices, precious stones, pearls and *objets d'art*; and in such quantity that everything used in the decoration of the Oratory of the Saviour was Indian and a part of the

FIG. 35

Fabric preserved in the Cluny Museum, Paris

Sacred Palace was called the Indous. From China came raw silk, spun silk, silken goods and porcelain. From Persia came beautiful carpets in an endless variety of design and colour, though blue, the heavenly colour, was the favourite in Byzantium. Wheat, salted fish, salt, honey, wax, caviare, furs, precious stones and slaves came from North Russia. Bulgaria sent flax, honey, fish and farm products. Worked and unworked metal came from Italy and Germany, as well as linen goods.

Disdainfully, Byzantium did not bother to seek commercial outlets but let the foreigner find his own way to her docks and warehouses. Few merchants journeyed outside the Empire either to buy or to sell. This was a serious mistake, for the day was to come when more active people supplanted her and exploited the Eastern market for themselves.

FIG. 36

Fabric preserved in the Kunstgewerbe Museum, Berlin. Found in the chest of St Annott, Archbishop of Cologne, which came from the old monastery of Sieburg, bearing the names of Lecapenus and Christopher, his son, 919–944

But for centuries she experienced no difficulty in selling her own finished goods at her own door. They were of infinite variety; but first and foremost were the silken goods. These were of all colours with, perhaps, a striking purple, a sombre violet, peach and pale green occurring most often. They bore many designs: sacred and profane, men and animals; some were embellished with embroidery, and in some gold and silver threads were interwoven. The silk from the Imperial workshop formed a separate category; some of it was striped with goats' hair. Until the sixth century Byzantium had been entirely dependent on China, the Indies, Japan, Persia and Syria for raw silk, but at some date between 527 and 565, according to Procopius of Caesarea, two monks brought some precious cocoons from China. They were bred and the Empire was soon producing nearly all the raw material it needed.

Embroidered and damask tapestries, simulating panther skins,

PLATE 8. *Mosaic in the chancel of San Vitale, Ravenna (6th century)*
Mosaic in St Apollinare Nuovo, Ravenna (6th century)

PLATE 9.
The resurrection of Lazarus. Byzantine bas relief in Ravenna

Mask on the sarcophagus of a Byzantine Emperor. Museum of Antiquities, Izmir

leather work and purple-dyed skins were celebrated products. The work of Byzantine smiths was in constant demand: shrines, reliquaries, altars, crosses, sacred vessels, dalmatics of blood red rubies and scintillating stones, articles of bronze inlaid with silver, in short all the products of 'the arts of fire and metal'. In good years figs, oranges, almonds, melons, mulberries, chestnuts, soaps and sponges were exported. Knowledge of this trade

FIG. 37

Reliquary in enamel and gold

has come down to us in a curious way, through philology: in the Balkan languages the names of all these articles are of Byzantine origin.

Byzantine goods were not only various, but their quality was unsurpassable. The whole of Europe was eager to get them. The Empire enjoyed a complete monopoly in the workmanship of gold and silver and in the manufacturing of silk and cloth.

The Basileus Romanus Lecapenus once gave to the King of Italy a chalice and several other articles made of glass. When the sun's rays fell on them they threw off red flame-like rays. On the silver casket sent ten years later by Constantine VII Porphyrogenitus to the Caliph, there was a picture of the Emperor himself in coloured glass mounted on gold.

Unfortunately few examples of such masterpieces from the

goldsmith's shop have come down to us. As regards tapestry, fate has been kinder. Until the seventeenth century the church at Auxerre preserved a precious yellow fabric which showed stylized lions on a violet background, majestic and serene, with tails erect. Siegburg Cathedral still has a similar piece. But the most famous of all was until quite recently at Aix-la-Chapelle. This famous 'fabric with elephants' has had a peculiar history. According to an inscription on it, it was made in a large workshop near the Sacred Palace. It was found in the tomb of Charlemagne and was probably put there by Otto III when he opened the tomb in the year 1000. Its background is purple and it shows in large tangential circles yellow elephants harnessed and caparisoned in blue.[1]

FIG. 38

Silk fabric from Charlemagne's tomb at Aix-la-Chapelle (Kunstgewerbe Museum, Berlin)

A cause and a consequence of Byzantium's economic importance was the ubiquity of her currency, the besant or nomisma. In the Middle Ages it held a position rather like that of the dollar in our time,

---

[1] This taste for rich, rare and costly material prevented the production of works of large dimensions, as Runciman pointed out in *Byzantine Civilization*. Without a good deal of capital at his disposal the Byzantine artist could rarely produce more than a miniature.

for it was the universally accepted medium of exchange. In China and Ceylon, merchants' money bags were full of these small coins which depicted the Basileus on one side, and on the other Christ, a cross, or the Theotokos; none other was acceptable. A sixth century writer called Kosmas, known also as 'the Navigator of the Indies' (he was probably a privateer), has told the following story. At the court of the King of Ceylon a Greek merchant called Zopathros met a Persian merchant. 'Which of your kings is the more powerful?' the king asked them. 'Mine,' declared the Persian, 'for he is the king of kings.' Zopathros said that there was no need to argue the matter, for the two kings were present. His companions were, of course, puzzled. 'Here you have both besants and dihrams,'[1] explained the Greek. 'Compare them.' The question was settled.

Byzantine bankers were very enterprising and to them was due much of the credit for the Empire's prosperity. Judging from the work of a seventh-century writer, John Moschos, Byzantium seems to have used payment clearances between one town and another six centuries before the West.

Naturally the Treasury profited from this wealth, which was fortunate for the Empire, for wars were costly. Thus the expedition undertaken in 468 against the Vandals of Africa required 113 ships and cost more than £4,500,000.

A duty of ten per cent was levied on all exports and imports. One of the customs points was at Abydos, the other at the entrance to the Black Sea. And a curious sight it must have been to see the customs officers, in their search for 'silk under linen or metal hidden under wax', pierce even the smallest packages with long, slender, sharp-pointed rods.

In a country which was comparatively wealthy transfer and inheritance taxes gave a fair yield.

Land tax and poll tax also formed an important part of the Imperial revenue, even though the patricians had legal exemption from the former and in practice did not pay the latter, for the Government found ways and means to make the *penes* pay. Taxes were made a village responsibility. If a peasant fled for any reason, his possessions were shared out amongst his fellow villagers together with his taxation forms. If there was no one

[1] The dihram was a Persian coin.

to inherit a holding, if, that is, there was a danger that the State might lose revenue, it too was divided up *volens nolens* amongst some of the more solvent village tax-payers. Even barren land was divided up, in proportion to people's wealth, and entered in their assessment. These practices gradually shaped village life: as the amount of taxation a man paid depended to some extent upon everyone else, there was a general desire for supervisory rights over one another, and an institution somewhat akin to joint ownership grew up.

In *The Constitution of the Later Roman Empire*, Bury gives us some interesting information about village life. The peasant retained in his own hands a vineyard and a vegetable garden, which were enclosed by sharply pointed fencing, and ploughed land. Livestock and pasture, on the other hand, were held in common. Twice a day, accompanied by a great deal of noise from bells and barking dogs, herds of cattle and flocks of sheep made their way through the village in charge of a paid shepherd. Wild animals, particularly wolves, were a constant threat. Sometimes at night they managed to get into the fold; and then woe betide the man responsible for stealing the watch dog, for he had to make amends for his own and the wild animals' crime. When everything was gathered in, the cattle were turned on to the arable fields.

The yield of two monopolies—purple fabrics and wheat—also enriched public funds. Only the State could trade in wheat. It was bought from the producers, stored in large warehouses called poundax, and sold to the bakers. But this monopoly had not only a fiscal aspect: it made possible the building up of reserves against lean years. In addition the government had the right of *annone*, a modification of the Roman *coemptio*: power, that is, to requisition standing corn.

Finally the State owned a great deal of property from which it secured considerable revenue.

Thus the Imperial budget was believed by many to have involved something like £220 million. According to the same estimates, from Constantinople alone the Treasury received each year £37 million in taxes on shops, market dues and customs duties. Some of the amounts bequeathed by certain sovereigns are not therefore entirely surprising. Basil I, for example, was said to have left £74 million to his successor.

III

THE BASILEUS GOES TO WAR

The Army

Byzantium always took great care of her army, yet it could not be said that she was militaristic. Learning and culture were always to be preferred to war. The ignorance of Michael II, the vulgar speech of Constantine Margarites and the strange accent of John Italus were held in great contempt. Cleverness and skill were the foremost qualities, diplomacy was the supreme art. The sword was the last resort, to be used only when intrigue and corruption had been fully tried. The aim was not to beat one's enemies but to divide them; at various times she set Venice against the Normans, the Italian cities against Frederick Barbarossa, Germany against France and the Kingdom of Sicily, Armenians against Arabs, and Russians against Bulgarians. Gold and honours were in this respect her most useful tools. To become a *patrice* or a *proedros*, to receive the golden diadem and the famous gown of embroidered silk which bore the effigy of the Basileus, to receive a portrait of the Emperor on the occasion of a coronation, what base deeds these ambitions have inspired—even amongst the Doges! There was an interesting section of the administration whose sole function was the collection of information about foreign peoples; the Office of Barbarians, it was called. Thus Byzantium also had her Intelligence Service, which briefed the Sacred Palace on the strength and weaknesses of each national group: emotions and interests to play on, desires to fulfil, fears to exploit, influential families to win over. This enabled her, most of the time, to attain her aims by peaceful means.

Even the clergy were expected to help. Suitably indoctrinated, groups of monks toured foreign countries to spread the good word and to seduce souls, particularly those of women —always more impressionable and mystical than men; orthodox religion must win new friends for the Empire. There were many examples of conversions of political importance: Crimean Goths, Caucasian Abasgians, Arabs from Himyar,

Ethiopians, Croats, Serbs, Moravians and Bulgarians amongst others.

Had Byzantium any intention of declaring war when, towards the end of the tenth century, tension between her and the Russian Prince Vladimir rose to a dangerous pitch? Definitely not, for she invited the Prince to pay a State visit to Constantinople and there did all she could to impress him. He was taken to St Sophia, shown the golden domes, made to attend divine worship, intoxicated with incense and dazzled by a thousand candles; but the climax came during mass when lovely winged creatures, beautifully clothed, flew slowly over the heads of the priests, singing, 'Holy! Holy! Holy! Our Lord God is eternal!' The bewildered pagans thought that they were witnessing some supernatural apparition, and were told in answer to their mumbled questions: 'If you were not ignorant of the Christian mysteries you would know that the angels themselves descend from heaven to celebrate mass with our priests', and, for ever won over, became willing tools in the hands of their astute partners.

FIG. 39
Oriental mercenary of the ninth and tenth centuries (after Hottenroth)

Nevertheless this diplomacy, this mixture of flattery and threat, presupposed a strong military arm; Byzantium did not neglect it. Her frontiers were protected by lines of fortresses in echelon, thus presenting a succession of barriers to the invader. The countryside bristled with strong points, important routes could be blocked at short notice and narrow defiles barred; strategic points were overlooked. As Charles Diehl[1] has said, one of the glories of Justinian was 'to have built over the steppes of Hodna, from Tunisia to the

[1] Diehl, *Byzance, grandeur et décadence*.

THE BASILEUS GOES TO WAR

banks of the Euphrates, from the mountains of Armenia to the banks of the Danube, a network of castella which, according to Procopius, saved the monarchy'.

Byzantine troops were the best paid in the world. In 809, when the Bulgarian King Kroum overran a Byzantine camp and took possession of £4,500,000 of gold, he did not realize that this was the pay of only the few battalions encamped along the Strymon.

Constantine VII, who always kept careful records, noted that the pay alone of the 14,459 men he sent to Crete amounted to a total of £1,500,000.

A corporal was paid £360 a year, a lieutenant £720, a captain £1,080 and a general £1,800 to £14,500, according to his class.[1] In addition to his pay the soldier could expect a share in any booty and an allocation of land. The latter was particularly valuable, as it was inviolable and free from taxation and inheritance duties. The grants never amounted to less than £725, or, in the case of cavalrymen and sailors who had served on ships carrying Greek fire, to less than £1,450. It is hardly surprising then that Harold needed a dozen young men to help him to carry

FIG. 40
Soldier of the sixth and seventh centuries (after Hottenroth)

---

[1] According to Gelzer (*Die Genesis der byzantinischen Themen verfassung*) pay was as follows:

Dekarkhes, in command of 10 men, 1 lb. of gold.
Pentekontarchai, in command of 50 men, 2 lb. of gold.
Kometes, in command of 200 men, 3 lb. of gold.
Generals commanded military districts and there were five classes of them—
Three 1st class generals, 40 lb. of gold each.
Three 2nd class generals, 30 lb. of gold each.
Five 3rd class generals, 20 lb. of gold each.
Three vice-admirals who commanded the three maritime districts of Cibyraioton, Samos and Aegaion Pelagos, were each paid 10 lb. of gold.
5th class generals, 5 lb. of gold each.

his gold back to Scandinavia when he had completed his service.

So firmly established was the custom of distributing part of the spoils amongst the soldiers that when Nicephorus the Logothete announced after the Bulgarian campaign of 809 that the entire booty would be handed over to the Treasury, a serious revolt ensued.

The military life had many other advantages. Quite significant are the following lines written in the tenth century. 'If we want our soldiers to set out with joyful and contented hearts, to risk their lives for the Holy Emperors and for the whole Christian community . . . they must have every consideration. They must not be despised, or ill-treated by vile tax collectors who render no service to the State. . . . It is unthinkable that they should be held under the jurisdiction of the ordinary courts, that they should be seen in chains like slaves and beaten with rods . . . these men who are the defenders and, with God's help the saviours of Christianity and who, one might say, are dying every day for the Holy Emperors.'

FIG. 41

Soldier of the Justinian guard (after Hottenroth)

Early in the history of the Empire, local power was handed over to the army.[1] The *strategos* was the military commander and governor of the region. *Turmarch, drungarios, kometes, katapan*

---

[1] But the absorption of power by the military was a gradual process which lasted nearly two centuries. At the beginning of the sixth century civil and military power were quite separate, but under the influence of Heraclius and his successors the military acquired more and more power so that by the end of the seventh century the army commander had complete local power and the theme, the area of command, was the unit of local government. This situation lasted until the Empire fell.

and *clisurarch* were all army officers.[1] The *protonotary* was the only civil official. His functions were tax collection and the administration of justice but his position in the nobility was low.

Administrative boundaries ignored economics and nationality; military requirements were the sole consideration. One result was that the names of the provincial districts, the 'themes', were arbitrary and apparently inconsequential. Some, like Dyrrachion, Nicopolis, Thessalonica, Seleucia and Lycandox were taken from the town in which the *strategos* resided, others came from a vague geographical term like Anatolia or Mesopotamia; sometimes a local celebrity provided a name and sometimes less obvious connections: the area from which Charsian, a hero of the Persian Wars, sprang was known as Charsios; the Bucellarian theme commemorated the Bucellarii Cataphracti, Optimate the Gothic Optimates, and Opsikion the Opsequentes of Marcus Aurelius.

FIG. 42

Grand Officer of the Empire

In peacetime there was one army corps in each 'theme', but in an emergency the units left their quarters and occupied camps along the possible invasion route. On the Syrian route, for example, there were a dozen such camps, extending from the Gulf of Nicodemia to Caesarea, the Cappadocian metropolis.

Few events were more colourful than the departure of an emperor for the battle area. Several chroniclers have left us detailed descriptions of the ritual which accompanied it. Let us then try to recapture the scene as a tenth century Basileus set out against the Saracen.

[1] The *Turmarch* administered the *turma*, a sub-district. *Drungarios* and *kometes* administered the *banda* or canton. The *katapan* was at the head of a foreign colony which enjoyed some of the privileges of the Imperial canton. The *clisurarch* commanded a *clisura*, or frontier fortress.

A Basileus leaves for the Wars

For many hours the look-out posts across the Bosphorus had been transmitting a message which had at last reached Chrysopolis. From there it was flashed to its destination and the Sacred Palace replied with the full power of its great beacon. The Emperor's armour, sword and shield were hanging on the gate at Chalcedon. In a moment the news had passed through the town: the army was about to set out against the Saracens. Once again the old, tested battalions were to cross the Taurus Mountains. Again the valleys and endless plains of Cilicia would resound with the clangour of Byzantine cavalry. Again in the burning solitudes of the Euphrates and the Orontes the heavy cataphracti regiments would measure themselves against the light squadrons of the Hamdanide.

In accordance with custom the Basileus had delegated to a high official, the Vicar, the power to act in his name, and now he gave the signal to depart. He left by the Xera gate, where great crowds were waiting to acclaim him, and soon reached his private port of Boucoleon, an entirely man-made harbour, with quays of marble. There, gently moving in the breeze, his galley was held in readiness. An assembly of magistrates, patricians, chamberlains and officials followed him on board. The day was beautiful and the light craft moved forward gently towards the Asian coast. The outline of Byzantium became hazy in the morning light. But thoughts about other matters than the beauty of the scenery besieged the Autocrator: here he was, leaving his excitable capital, where riots sprang up so quickly and which always remained the object of the barbarians' plans. He got up and, facing the town, made three great signs of the cross. 'Lord Jesus,' he cried, 'I leave this city in Thy hands. Shield it from all misfortunes and calamities. Protect it from civil war and from the attack of the barbarians. Make it impregnable, that no one may harm it, for it is in Thee that we put our trust. Thou art the Lord of pity, the Father of compassion, the God of all consolations. Have pity on us! Save us! Shield us from temptation now and forever! Amen.'

The Bosphorus was soon crossed; the galley entered the Gulf

of Nicomedia and moved towards the shore. Gradually on the Asian coast a multitude of strange dots appeared, all of them red. They came closer, grew larger, and at last were recognizable. Here were animals, more than a thousand of them! Horses, donkeys and mules, all harnessed from head to hoof in scarlet. They were lined up as if on parade and, indeed, the Basileus inspected his animals before he inspected his troops. There were hunters and pack-horses, finely built animals and heavy ones, thoroughbred mounts and sturdy beasts of burden. They were gifts—compulsory ones, to be sure. A grave official, the 'logothete of herds', 'piously and in the fear of God and in all sincerity' kept up to date a register of offerings; and as they were all 'willingly given' it was well understood that no one, not even the great nobles, could withdraw. This business-like list of contributors took on a poetic resonance with such names as *Kometes* of the Stable, *Sacellary*, *Chartulary* of the Themes, Public *Logothete*, *Zygostates*, *Genikon*, *Kometes* of the Scholars, *Kometes* of the Excubitors, *Kometes* of the Hicanates or Immortals.

The church, too, had had to open its stables: the 'most holy monasteries' had provided, shod and loaded 100 horses, the college of metropolitans and that of archbishops 52 mules each. Was it to take the bitterness out of this imposition or had the odour of sanctity passed from man to quadruped? Whatever the reason, these ecclesiastical beasts always received favoured treatment. They formed the head of the convoy—they even preceded the Emperor—and were not branded with the Imperial seal.

Conscripts that they were, these animals all wore the same uniform, rather striking no doubt, but camouflage was not yet considered essential. It consisted of a red cover made of short-nap cloth from the Imperial workshops, a purple horse-cloth from the Curator of Trichines in Lydia, and 'pantaloons' to protect them from insect bites. Military status brought them all sorts of advantages. If they fell ill *en route* they would be looked after very carefully in special stables. Every evening they had their temperatures taken by a dignified official, the *epiktes*. If they were too heavily laden next morning the culprit had his head shorn.

However many animals had been gathered together, the Basileus was never satisfied and wherever he went he harassed the local authorities for more carriers. No wonder that every protonotary prayed that the Imperial procession would pass through his neighbour's territory! The Emperor indeed did not scorn personal comfort and until the very last moment was accompanied by an impressive amount of baggage.

He did not intend, for example, to give up the pleasures of the table. Thus 100 horses at least were needed for transporting his silverware, cooking utensils and food. In addition 500 horses, 50 cows, 200 foals, 100 geese and 100 sheep and goats were driven along until they were needed for the pot. Fresh fish were provided by a team of highly skilled fishermen brought specially for this purpose from Tembri in distant Opsikion. And the Basileus certainly expected to find wine and oil on his table and on restricted days at least beans, cheese, little fish in Saumur wine and caviare. But he did not limit himself to these things and would not hesitate *en route* to requisition large quantities of poultry and vegetables. That is why the 'Instructions' gravely reminded the Chief of Table and the *oikiarch* never to forget to take nets for carrying birds and wooden bowls for watering the chickens.

Nor did the Basileus intend to eschew the pleasure of dressing up, even if he had no other audience than that of soldiers and backward subjects. He took with him an incalculable number of shirts of fine silk, satin over-garments, decorative scarves, dressing-gowns, ceremonial garments and night attire as well as *scaramangia* of various designs and colours. He had a dozen swords for ceremonial and everyday wear and as many golden pomelled saddles. He was always in a cloud of incense—cinnamon, mastic, musk, ambergris; he burnt aromatic pellets and used large amounts of penetrating perfume. A beautiful lantern stood outside his tent. Inside were chandeliers, silver bowls, metal kettles and fine tapestries. All these things were packed with much toil into immense chests of purple copper with iron fittings; 30 horses were needed to carry them and they were anxiously guarded by *vestiarites* and *kitonites*, his personal servants.

Then there was the serious matter of his health to attend to!

And so more horses were mobilized for the complete pharmacy which the Basileus took with him: elixirs, plasters, medicinal herbs, healing oils and antidotes to the poison of serpents, dragons and scorpions. Nor was spiritual welfare forgotten. A mobile library accompanied the expedition; it included serious and frivolous works: books on strategy and history, works on the interpretation of dreams, such as the one called *Oneirokritis* by Artemidorus, books about the seasons of the year and the weather, celestial phenomena, books of devotion, homilies, prayers, etc.

But the moment came when enemy territory was reached and his comfort had to be sacrificed. Then, sometimes with a deep sigh, he left most of his possessions with the last protonotary and proceeded with only the 'absolute essentials'. These, however, included a Turkish bath or 'Scythian *tzerga*', a sort of leather device for steam baths 'prepared the Armenian way', a collection of basins, braziers and the bricks of a fireplace, beds for his suite and a private chapel with a portable altar, holy icons and all the sacred accessories. One can therefore understand the concern of a Basileus for his animals and the care with which he usually scrutinized them.

FIG. 43

Altar (from a manuscript)

This having been done, he went on to inspect his troops, which were scattered in a series of camps. First that of Malagina, the rallying point of the Anatolians and Thracians; then that of Dorylaeum, the present-day Eski-Shehir on the Thymbros, the tributary of the Sangarius which Godfrey de Bouillon was to cross in 1067 after his victory over the Seljuk Turks.

As the sovereign approaches, everyone renders homage

according to his rank: officers dismount, while ordinary soldiers, cavalry excepted, of course, throw themselves to their knees. Then the August One addresses a few paternal words to them. 'Soldiers, I hope that all is well with you. My children, how are your wives, my daughters? How are your children?' And all reply with the conventional words 'In the radiance of your majesty, oh Basileus, we your slaves are well'. The Basileus makes the concluding remark: 'Glory be to God who will continue to hold us in his safe keeping'.

At Dorylaeum, the first part of the journey usually ended. Other camps would be inspected the next day. In the evening his tents—pavilions is perhaps a more suitable word—were set up. They were furnished in the height of luxury, with elaborate chairs, inlaid tables, lustrous coverings, soft purple silk cushions and fur rugs. One tent served as dining room, the other as bedroom. Ritual demanded that when he reached the halting place he should find them already set up; as each morning they could not be taken down until he had departed, work in his service demanded great speed.

In the evening, according to custom, the Emperor usually invited the general staff to supper and on each occasion ceremonial clothes were distributed. Time passed quickly with anecdotes and jokes, usually at the expense of the Saracens.

Just before nightfall another purposeful ritual was performed. The *Idikos* handed a torch to the *Drongary* of the *Vigiles* as a symbol of his responsibility. A hundred *hetairae* under a *hetairarch* covered the immediate approaches and a hundred scouts were posted a little farther out. The Emperor gave his guests permission to depart and retired to his bedroom. Henceforth anyone moving about would need the password—the name of the Saviour perhaps, or that of his mother, the divine Theotokos, or perhaps the name of the Archangel Michael, *Archstrategos* of the heavens. There was no further communication with the Autocrator; no one, not even a eunuch of the wardrobe or his valet, was allowed to penetrate the circle of hanging shields. Patrols moved about constantly until daybreak and anyone trying to get through would be seized immediately and put in chains.

Even greater precautions were taken in enemy territory. The

THE BASILEUS GOES TO WAR

palace staff which had hitherto mounted guard was replaced by *akrites*, the famous frontier sentries. In their thousands they took up positions near the Emperor, before, behind and at his side, while the *protostrator*, the *kometes* of the stable, with three equerries and three saddled horses, slept at the door of his tent.

Summer nights in Asia Minor are short. The Emperor was up at dawn and the signal to depart was soon given. Before long he had reached the shores of Lake Tatta, entered Cappadocia and arrived at the great camp at Caesarea, where the famous troops from Central Asia Minor had recently assembled.

There, at the foot of Mount Argeus, from which, it was said, the two seas could be seen, the *drungarios*, the *turmarchs* and the *centarchs* had shouted their last orders and strange, wild music shattered the silence: raucous and frightening trumpet calls, the rhythmic clashing of cymbals, the staccato rolling of drums and wild war songs. The Basileus had the whole of his army within his sight and it was ready to move.

How many nationalities, races and types were gathered there! They had not even the Greek language in common, for many spoke no Greek; only the same religious faith united them. There

FIG. 44

Soldier of the ninth and tenth centuries (after Hottenroth)

were peasants from Thrace and Macedonia, former prisoners from Cappadocia, Lycaonia and the Black Sea coast, Armenians from the very frontier of the Christian world, renowned for their courage. And there were idolatrous Russians, of whom Byzantium was very proud. They were commanded by their own officers and accompanied by interpreters. They were 'as tall as palm-trees' and covered in armour from head to foot.

There were legends about them. It was said that a few hundred of them were worth an army; that they had never been known to give themselves up but fell rather on their own swords. The first of them had arrived not long ago in strange craft carved out of a single tree trunk and now treaties made with their czars put them regularly at the disposal of the Empire. Byzantium paid for them at the rate of 10, 12 or even 15 golden coins a month—say £180 to £220—as well as hiring premiums and other gratuities.

There, dressed in dark furs and animal skins, were the ferocious Slavesians and Toulmates; the mounted *cataphracti* with shining breastplate invulnerable to javelin and sword; the ranks of Khazars, Phargans, Iberians, Mardaïtes, Arabs, Turks. There were Normans from Scandinavia and Italy, of whom there were many encamped colonies throughout the Empire.[1]

For the Empire relied heavily on mercenaries. Conscription was no longer regarded very favourably, as too many recruits, dragged from the plough, had been of the poorest quality. Soon the administration granted exemptions and permitted buying out. Moreover, the Basileus had greater confidence in mercenary troops for they would take no part in political life. Indeed, high command and military honours were usually bestowed upon foreigners. Finally the cosmopolitan nature of his army flattered the Emperor's vanity: he was indeed a universal sovereign.[2]

The system had its drawbacks. For one thing, professionals had an inflated sense of their own value. Again, they considered themselves above ordinary rules and did not always deign to obey; often one had to negotiate with them and compromise. Their cupidity was proverbial; sometimes the Greek communities feared their arrival more than that of the enemy from whom they were supposed to be protecting them. Everything depended

---

[1] The Mardaïtes of Syrian origin were established along the Ionian Sea and in the Peloponnese; the Mardaïtes from Lebanon on the coast south of Anatolia. The Turks were on the Vardar and the Arabs on the Euphrates. The Slavs were lightly sprinkled everywhere; in Macedonia, on the Strymon, at the gates of Thessalonica, in Thessaly and in Bithynia.

[2] The composition of the army varied from one century to another, of course, for it reflected the national composition of the Empire. When the Byzantines were firmly established in the Balkans it was largely European; as they fell back on Asia Minor it became overwhelmingly Asiatic.

upon their commander, for only a strong man was able to exact obedience and orderly conduct.

Armament and equipment were varied and represented the last word in technical development. There were movable siege towers, apparatus for setting fire to harbours, *testudos* on four wheels, *ballista*, catapults, crossbows worked by pulley and cable, iron-clad battering rams, machines for throwing rocks, bombs of inflammable oil, movable and articulated ladders, giant slings and gigantic traps. Above all, there was Greek fire, Byzantium's secret weapon. Barbarians and Saracens would have dearly liked to know how to manufacture this infernal mixture of inflammable materials, but the secret remained jealously guarded. It was Byzantium's best defensive weapon and had often saved her from invasion. In the ninth century when Prince Igor had forced the Bosphorus and all seemed lost, the engineers had flung themselves upon their pyrophorous syphons and manipulated them with such skill that in an instant, under a torrent of Greek fire, the 10,000 craft were in flames. . . .

Assured that all was ready for the great campaign, the Basileus slowly rose in the saddle and made a majestic sign with his hand. Then slowly he set out along the road to Taurus, the road which led to those wild and devastated lands where only the *akrite* lived, inaccessible to fear and enemy alike, the road which led away from the orderly world, beyond which nothing remained but the enemy and war.

War

As the result of the discovery of a tenth-century treatise on tactics we have a good deal of information concerning the way in which Byzantium conducted its defensive wars. The official teaching stressed mobility; indeed one has the impression that everything else should be sacrificed to mobility and the element of surprise. 'If you move rapidly,' say the instructions, 'above all if the work of your scouts, your intelligence and your couriers is reliable, you can be certain of defeating a battalion with a detachment, an army with only a battalion.' And in 25 chapters with suggestive headings the work goes on to explain the measures to be taken.

The first step is to organize the frontier thoroughly. Night and day, from high vantage points with a wide field of vision, 3,000 or 4,000 yards apart, and connected by a system of signalling, the *akrites*, the famous hand-picked sentries, must survey the plain, undertake deep reconnaissance, question travellers, peasants, merchants and caravans. If there are disturbing reports of troop concentrations, the commander must immediately clear the area facing the potential enemy. That is to say, with or without the villagers' consent, he encloses men, women, animals, fodder and harvests of the threatened zone behind fortified lines.

If the enemy starts to move, the commander must quickly send his scouts to trail him. Let us follow them as they carry out one of their tasks. After having been blessed they leave by night under a *turmarch*, each with a day's supply for man and horse, and gallop till dawn. When the first rays of the sun appear, they dismount; the men rest and the horses feed. At nine o'clock they move off again, silent as shadows. When they reach a suitable eminence they climb it; in particular they are looking for clouds of dust which might indicate moving troops, or trodden grass, particularly near fords and likely stopping places. At sunset they approach the Saracen camp; during the night they creep close, waiting for the first noise to announce reveille. From now on, without his knowing it, the Saracen will have them at his heels and on his flanks, well disposed in groups of six. Soon, possessed of much information, they turn about and make straight for camp where they will immediately report to the commander.

If the latter feels himself strong enough to attack, the treatise suggests that the Arabs should either be surprised at rest or ambushed on the mountainous frontier.

In the former case, the assault should be made on some precise point, preferably the baggage and victuals. If at the same time a diversionary attack is arranged, nine times out of ten he will be able to capture the camels, intent on grazing and perhaps even still loaded. Immobilized and without food, the enemy is an easy prey.

If he decides to prepare an ambush, then he must hide the heavy infantry on the wooded heights of the two sides while leaving the light infantry and artillery openly on the road as bait.

The Arabs, however, may be much superior in numbers. In such an event, they must not be attacked but left free to do their looting. Only on their way back, when loaded with booty, oppressed by fatigue and without look-outs, they cross the mountains again, should the commander fall on them and decimate them.

Whatever the case, one particular ruse was strongly recommended in the manual. Some men should be disguised as peasants or women and move along the road, driving their animals before them. Arab soldiers would certainly be detailed to follow them, so they should simulate flight; but they must suddenly turn, draw their swords and cut down the bewildered enemy.

In most of the territory the Byzantines were likely to fight in, the question of water was of particular importance. The smallest source, the tiniest stream, should be the object of the most careful attention. It is even recommended that in arid regions one-tenth of the strength should be detailed to carry water bottles and keep the front line supplied during battle.

Much space in the treatise is devoted to the problem of the town which is about to be besieged. At the danger signal the commander must fill his cisterns and granaries, summon the peasants from the fields and make a waste land round the town. Springs must be blocked up, crops, pastures and fruit trees and even thatched roofs must be burnt, cut or otherwise destroyed. The more barren the desert, the sooner the besiegers will move off. Once invested, many manoeuvres are recommended, amongst them the following. At night a noisy attempt to break out should be made. At the same time, and at a point in the ramparts directly opposite, several well-mounted men, each carrying four empty baskets, should rush out to get provisions.

No companion volume on offensive war has been found. It is possible that none was written, for few campaigns were undertaken just to destroy an enemy army. The aim was usually to sack and to loot, and as it was in fortified towns that the greatest opportunities for theft and outrage could be found, the conduct of a siege was the principal feature of aggressive war. And here there were not many differences between Eastern and Western practices. Day after day the assailant kept up a bombardment of stones; and as this became effective only in the long run, he was soon the prey of boredom. Boredom might be relieved by testing the town's defences from time to time, but that meant exposing oneself to a thousand disagreeable projectiles, such as burning oil, flaming javelins, pieces of rock and hand grenades, not to mention the risk of being harpooned with iron hooks. So other distractions had to be found, and perhaps it was in this domain that an Oriental siege took on a special colour because of the cruelty and perversity that characterized it. For example, a living donkey might be fired from a ballista; the fun came from watching its contortions in the air. The bodies of enemies could be quietly collected from the moat at night and decapitated; the pleasantry consisted in fixing a head on each of the points of the stockade and listening to the screams of the garrison at dawn. There was an improvement on this game: the corpses were divided into arms, legs, heads and trunks, loaded into the machines and catapulted over the ramparts. With a little luck the faces would arrive still recognizable and then there would be the pleasant howls of grief of the relatives. Hunger also frequently attacked a besieging army, for it was impossible to live off the country if the scorched earth policy had been put into effect. Consequently the investment of a starving town by a starving army was not an unknown situation.

Belligerents would use any expedient which might cut short a siege and many examples are to be found in the chronicles. The following, which was used by Byzantium in the tenth century, was particularly enjoyed by connoisseurs. Tired of conducting a seemingly endless siege, the Byzantine general Nicephorus Phocas told the Aleppo garrison that he was ready to start negotiations. The message was favourably received and the next day representatives came through the lines bearing a white flag. Nicephorus received them in the customary manner: he caused them to lie on the ground, lightly poked them with his foot, had them embrace his knees and then offered them refreshment. Finally he put forward his proposal: 'Let me march my army through your walls. I will harm neither your lives nor your goods and the matter will be settled.' The delegates retired for consultation, but when they returned the next morning with a favourable reply, Nicephorus feigned dreadful anger, saying that his spies had warned him of a trap for his army. Concealed troops were going to surprise it and cut it to pieces. The delegates were dumbfounded. How could they have such a design, they asked, considering the state the town was in and the lack of fit men. Let him only look at a plan of the town and of its defences. Here it was. Let him see for himself. And Nicephorus did look! The next day he was in a position to attack the weakest point, and captured and sacked the town.

When treachery failed, the assailants had to wait until famine, epidemics or wear and tear on the ramparts brought a decision. But how inconsequential they were! For days and days they had been stealing stealthily about, perhaps camouflaged, hiding their movements in a hundred ways. But when the time for the assault at last had arrived, there they were proclaiming their intentions to the besieged! They set up a terrible din, noisy enough to awaken the dead, not to mention sleeping sentries. If it was a Byzantine army, the drums rolled, the trumpets sounded and the Hymn to the Virgin surged up from the ranks. From both sides a frantic rush towards the ramparts followed. At this point a strange incident might occur. Old Saracen women looking like witches, fleshless and toothless, sometimes climbed to the top of a tower in full view of the besieging army and there, cursing dreadfully, undressed. Then they gave up their naked bodies to gestures and movements of a precise obscenity. Often this was more than the pious Byzantines could bear; fearful that they were witnessing a scene from hell they stopped dead. Indeed, if there was no cynic in the ranks capable of firing a few arrows at the lascivious hags, the whole offensive was checked. But if the attackers, with the Cross at their head, had arrived at the foot of the ramparts, then methodical operations started.

First the light artillery sent over a hail of stones and other missiles which made the defenders' position untenable. Next the heavy artillery pounded the stonework with rocks and metalled battering rams. Then, under cover of a barrage of Greek fire from the siege towers, the engineers rushed into the moat and undermined the wall. When it was on the point of collapse, it was propped up with beams and buttresses of dry wood. When their work was finished they set fire to the timberwork; the wall fell into the moat and filled it. The infantry had withdrawn a short distance and now came back in force, surging into the breach. The climax of the attack was reached; the town was overrun.

Now the attackers gave themselves up to looting and raping. No one held back. Here young girls were dragged by their hair towards some quiet corner, while there the arms of old men who had been trying to protect their possessions were severed by a swift blow with a sword. Everywhere blood was spilled, fires were started. At long last the reward for the boredom and monotony of the siege had arrived!

Enamelled silver vases, cloths of sumptuous silk, vessels of gold and silver, ewers of pure crystal, pouches full of diamonds, cups of engraved bezoar, coffers full of valuable arms, gem-studded daggers, inkstands of gold, silver, sandalwood, ebony and ivory, bladders of musk, porcelain eggs full of rare perfumes, mirrors of all kinds, chessboards, material of chequered silk and gold, damask tapestries, embossed shields, coats of mail by the thousand: such was the nature of the booty from a large town. When Aleppo fell in the tenth century the Byzantines seized four million dirhems in minted silver alone—a fabulous fortune! Nothing was respected, nothing was spared. The Alhallabah, Shiekh Eddauleh's palace, contained a thousand and one treasures; it was, indeed, the subject of poetry. But when the soldiers reached it they stripped the roof of its gilded tiles and set fire to everything they could not take away. In a few moments this marvel of Saracen art, of richness and elegance, was a mass of cinders. What pleasure there was in revenge and destruction! In pumping water into the great vats of olive oil, for instance, so that they would overflow and destroy the harvest stored nearby!

When this first orgy was over, it was time to put an official stamp on the change of occupation. This was done, not as in modern days by the changing of national flags in the town hall or elsewhere, but by various depredations in the places of

FIG. 45

Central part of an ivory triptych of the tenth century (Vatican Museum)

worship. The Christians would use the mosques as stables and solemnly burn the pulpits, generally of sycamore inlaid with mother-of-pearl. A Mohammedan victory, on the other hand, saw Arab mares stabled in the churches; the altars would be turned into mangers and the sacred vessels into drinking troughs; dervishes would dress themselves up in priestly garments and cut themselves stout staffs from processional crosses.

As for the civilians, when they had managed to survive hunger, typhus, cholera, plague and the sacking of the town, they were either led into captivity or sold to slave merchants who, by now, were buzzing about like flies. It was essential that they should not be allowed to remain in the town, a potential fifth column; so it sometimes happened that they were simply put to the sword. A Cilician town had obtained an honourable surrender in recognition of its bravery, and its garrison, still bearing arms, was filing past its conquerors. Some Byzantine soldiers noticed a group of attractive Saracen girls and tried to carry them off, whereupon husbands and fathers went to their defence. No more was necessary: within a few moments the whole population had been massacred. Starvation was perhaps a more painful death. When Anarzabe surrendered in the tenth century, the women, children and old people were thrown outside the walls. As the surrounding countryside had been completely ravaged, this meant that they were condemned to death by slow starvation.

Then, when all the booty had been assembled, when it was impossible to load one more ounce of gold on to horse, mule or donkey, the victorious army returned to its base, bringing in its rear a long string of cattle and bound prisoners. The possibility of occupying the conquered country was hardly considered. How could it be? The country was devastated. At the most a few detachments were left in key positions. And what would happen next? The following year the defeated would move forward in large numbers and overwhelm the feeble detachments which had been left behind. Lost ground would be reconquered. Enemy territory would be invaded, besieged, pillaged. Then they too would come back laden with booty, leaving small detachments behind. There was an eternal pendulum movement. It is not difficult to imagine the destitute condition to which the frontier regions were reduced.

As an example, the following story has come down to us. One day a strange detachment of several thousand men arrived outside the tent of the Emir of Aleppo, the famous Sheikh Eddauleh. The mahdi leading them explained that he had come to offer his services in the war against the accursed *Roumi* (Christian). He had preached holy war, and gathered a band of volunteers together; then to reach the battle area they had crossed Asia Minor, Armenia and the Taurus Mountains. The Sheikh was pleased with these reinforcements, and sent them straight to Cilicia, to Massissa, which was at that time besieged by the Byzantines. But the intervening country was so devastated—

FIG. 46

Lintel of a door at Dana (sculptured stone)

people were eating carrion—that, becoming famished too, these 'globe-trotting' warriors had to disband, some joining the forces of the Bouïd Sultan, while others journeyed over the mountain and valley back to their distant homeland.

Sometimes, however, the operations achieved permanent results: entire provinces were conquered and treaties of submission were made. But this was certainly exceptional.

An estimate of the size of these invasion armies would be useful; but on that score we can be certain of nothing. It is not that the chroniclers are silent on the subject, but rather that their evidence is suspect. Thus when the Arabs described a Byzantine army as being 400,000 strong, they would be making excuses for a campaign which turned out to be disastrous for them. A figure of 150,000 to 200,000 is probably nearer the truth.

Homecoming

The return of a Basileus to Byzantium after a prolonged expedition against 'the children of Hagar'[1] was no mean affair. It was a grand festival, and the occasion of a minute ceremonial, beside which our modern victory parades seem very shabby affairs.

During his march through the themes of Asia the Conqueror had already experienced a real triumph. Eager throngs had hurried up to admire the prodigious booty: the massive gates, iron-studded and inlaid with mother-of-pearl, taken from captured Saracen towns; vases, cloth, innumerable precious stones, golden crosses and ciboria wrested from infidel hands, the prisoners and the long lines of roped animals.

But in Byzantium quite different ovations awaited him, noisy and fatiguing. So that he could face them, he was first of all allowed some rest; having reached one of his towns on the coast of Asia Minor the Basileus stayed there a while, bathed and changed into ceremonial dress. This halt—the *messalogon*—sometimes lasted a long time. Theophilus, for instance, on one occasion had to remain idle for seven days until all his trophies were assembled. As he was getting bored he summoned his senators and, more particularly, their wives, to entertain him.

When he had recovered his energy, the Emperor boarded his vessel, which had been held in readiness and, accompanied by the fleet, set out for the port of Hebdomon on the European coast.

On the quayside an assembly of high dignitaries awaited him; the town prefect, senators and patricians. Some were dressed entirely in white, others entirely in red. At a sign from the silentiary and in order of seniority, each group approached to adore Christ's representative on earth. He for his part deigned to listen to the praise and leaning slightly forward from the height of his horse spoke the conventional words: 'How are you, my eminent children? How are your wives, my daughters? etc. . . .'

Then, under the watchful eyes of the prepository and the chief of catastase, the procession formed and moved off.

He was the central figure in numerous ceremonies. An incal-

[1] This was a name Byzantium sometimes used for the Saracens.

PLATE 10. *A mystic relief on the wall of St Mark's, Venice*

The lion and the bull (Cimitile)

PLATE 11. Mosaics from the old Monastery of the Holy Saviour in Chora, Byzantium: (above) the tympanum of the Exonarthex; (below) the Marriage at Cana. Early 14th century

culable number of times the Emperor stopped, prayed, lit candles and completely changed his clothing. At the Church of St John the Evangelist he changed his helmet for the tiara, covered his armour with the *scaramangion* of purple silk, adorned his wrists with golden bracelets and put golden stockings and gloves upon his limbs.

At the Abramite monastery he put on a garment of gold, edged with large-sized pearls, placed the *caesarikion* upon his head and buckled on a new sword. In the Temple of the Most Holy Theotokos in the Forum he had to assume the silken *debetesion* and the golden *chlamys*; on his feet he must place the purple *campagia*. He was constantly offered crowns, which he had to put on.

Behind him came an endless string of officials; in front, at the ritual distance, pranced the barbarian horsemen of the guard, armed with lance and sword, the eunuch cubicularies and protospatharies, furnished with halberds, each one wearing gilded armour. A thick crowd lined the route of the procession, their flags, flamoula and flowers adding yet more colour to the scene.

As the triumphal march was about to start, the Empress arrived before her glorious lord. She knelt and he, getting down from his horse, raised her up, kissed her forehead and bestowed tender greetings upon her.

Before arriving at the Golden Gate, the procession reached some tents. There the principal Arab sheikhs waited in chains in the midst of a glittering booty; as soon as the Emperor had passed, they were carried on litters in the procession.

And now the famous Gate was reached.[1] From the time of Theodosius II all Byzantine conquerors had passed beneath this triumphal triple arch of marble. The Basileus dismounted. Three times he prostrated himself towards the East and worshipped God. The tumult died away and there was perfect silence. Then the Unique One remounted and entered the centre gates, the famous golden gates which were opened only in his honour. Children ran forward; they sang songs and threw him flowers.

All around him were strange soldiers with short hair and carefully shaven beards, dressed in little robes of black wool;

---

[1] The Golden Gate was built by Theodosius II to celebrate the victory of Constantine the Great over Maximus the Pagan.

they had velvet diadems on their heads, wore necklaces of roses and toyed with their kerchiefs. They shouted in unison: 'Glory to God who has magnified the Ruler of the Romans. Glory to the Holy Trinity for our glorious master has returned victorious. Welcome, oh most noble and victorious monarch.' These men represented the Factions and they shouted in this way for several hours.

Now the town prefect and his deputy prostrated themselves. With outstretched hands they offered him two crowns: one of laurel for the head and the other of pearls, gems and gold, for the right arm. This action was perhaps not entirely disinterested, for the Emperor had in exchange to give them a greater weight of gold.

The procession then moved into the Mese, the triumphal avenue that was set with gigantic paving stones. What processions had passed that way and what gruesome relics! For example, the head of Denzerichos, son of Attila, killed by Arapastos, on the point of a sword, and the hand of the tyrant Phocas, also affixed to a sword. By order of the Praetor the whole route had been splendidly decorated. Everywhere were sweet-smelling flowers—rosemary, myrtle, roses, etc.—to drive away the normal odours; vividly-coloured stuffs: enormous Babylonian tapestries depicting men and animals, and incomparable Persian embroideries, were hung out and entirely hid the buildings. On every balcony precious objects glittered: vases of gold and silver, incense-burners, costly weapons. The road had been carefully swept, sprayed with scented water and then strewn with leaves. Candelabra were lit, and their hundred thousand lights, together with the sun's rays, gave the procession a strange glitter.

The procession was now in the Sigma district, or Crescent, so called because of its shape. Then it passed through the Xerolophon, or Forum Arcadii, to the Bous, the Forum of the Ox. For a long time a gigantic bronze animal had stood there which was used for the roasting of political criminals; in it the tyrant Phocas was roasted alive. It was finally pulled down by Heraclius in order to mint the metal or, as people said, to avoid at the hands of his successor the death he had meted out to Phocas. Then the procession came to the Capitolion, dedicated to ancient

THE BASILEUS GOES TO WAR

Rome, then to the Philadelphion, the Forum of Theodosius or the great Taurus square, the Artopoleum or bread market, the Forum of Constantine, and finally into the Augusteum. There the Emperor was welcomed by the Patriarch and his clergy. He dismounted. He went into a little chapel where he changed his clothing. Then he crossed the threshold of St Sophia. At each doorway and in each room new ceremonies awaited him. He was preceded by priests who held the most venerable objects on high: the labarum, the principal sacred vases, the standards and flags of the Church, the great sceptres, the golden flammoula and especially the True Cross, all studded with jewels.

When the Emperor emerged from St Sophia he recrossed the Augusteum and stopped in front of the great bronze doors of the Palace, facing the Daphne Pavilion. There in the open air a strange ceremony awaited him. The setting was curious: in the foreground, a throne; on one side the great golden organ; on the other the *sentzon*—a golden throne glittering with precious stones. Behind it all was the True Cross, set with jewels. Slowly the Basileus ascended the steps to his throne and made the sign of the cross. Immediately, the Factions shouted in a resounding voice: 'Only one is holy!' The city magistrates approached and presented new golden bracelets to the sovereign, who slipped them over his arms and rose. Now everyone was quiet, for the Triumphant One was going to speak to the multitude which filled the square. In a carefully prepared speech, with great deliberation, he listed his victories: battles won and towns captured. He described the booty taken, the seized treasure and the captured standards. Finally he gave the names and the number of his captives. In the way laid down by etiquette the crowd murmured with pride and applauded each item on the list.

FIG. 47

Tiberius Constantine, sixth century, and Justinian II, seventh century

Then the Emperor descended from the throne and remounted his horse. He passed the long porticos or galleries of Achilles, skirted the Zeuxippos baths, crossed the Hippodrome and reached the side doors of the Palace. Then the outside ceremonies were over and he could go to his apartments. But his hour of freedom had not yet come. Until the night was ended ceremonies awaited him within: presents, gratuities, the distribution of purses of gold and ceremonial clothes to the senators, songs and mime dances by the Factions, banquets for several hundred guests in the great Triclinium of Justinian, concerts, plays, games.

It usually went on till dawn set him free. More than one sovereign must have echoed the words of the Basileus who had said, 'If I had let myself be defeated I would not have been so tired today'.

IV

THE EMPIRE OF *COUPS D'ÉTAT*

Revolution was in Byzantium the most frequently used method of changing the government, to the point that it was accepted as constitutional; which is not surprising when we remember that there was no other means of acquiring power and that, moreover, there was no ostracism to limit the number of potential dictators. The figures are eloquent. Of 109 sovereigns, 65 were assassinated, 12 died in convent or prison, 3 died of hunger, 18 were castrated or had their eyes put out, their noses or hands cut off, and the rest were poisoned, suffocated, strangled, stabbed, thrown down from the top of a column or ignominiously hunted down. In 1,058 years there were 65 revolutions of palace, street or barracks and 65 dethronements. So one can say of Byzantium, too, that it was an absolute monarchy tempered by assassination.

No study of Byzantine life would be complete without an account of a *coup d'état*. Why choose that attempted by Nicephorus Phocas in the tenth century? The answer is difficult. Each being marked by deceit, violence, love and ambition, all in fact resemble one another. But Nicephorus puts one in mind of Napoleon—he has been called the Byzantine Napoleon—and here also there was a Josephine and a Barras.

In 963 Romanus II died, leaving two minors as his successors. The situation at once appeared dangerous, as is often the case at the beginning of a regency. Two strong characters, a eunuch and a beautiful woman, faced one another. The eunuch Bringas was prime minister; he was cold, energetic, unscrupulous and had already led the Empire for more than ten years. The woman was the young widow Theophano. She was twenty years old, she had green eyes, a beautiful face, a lovely voice—but let us not be carried away: she had already assassinated her father-in-law, driven out her mother-in-law, imprisoned her sisters-in-law, poisoned her husband, and was prepared to do anything else necessary to secure supreme power. But she was a woman, and to succeed she needed a lover: hence the third character. Alas! he was neither young nor goodlooking. He was fifty years old and far from tall; his olive-coloured skin was burnt by the sun of Asia Minor. 'He is broader than he is tall,' it was said, 'and he has the hindquarters of a Hun and a grizzly beard.' And much trouble Theophano had to take to seduce him, for he wanted to retire to a seminary. He mixed only with monks, spoke only of God, macerated himself day and night and above all avoided women. But Theophano wanted to win him over because he was a general and a victorious one. He was venerated by his troops and he bore a name which was respected through the Empire, Nicephorus Phocas.

When the curtain rises, Bringas and Theophano are in Byzantium, smiling at one another in public and trying to destroy one another in secret. Nicephorus is in the country, at the camp of Tzamandos, sheltering in the midst of his army or what is left of it, for he has just completed a hard campaign in Cilicia. There are no signs of the coming storm. But one day, wishing to take counsel with her lover, Theophano sends him a message in code, and he hastens to Byzantium.

FIG. 48

Decoration from a manuscript of the eleventh century (private collection)

Events then moved quickly. By leaving his troops, Nicephorus had lost his best protection, and Bringas was not the man to overlook such an opportunity. He convoked the Regency Council and proposed that Phocas should be seized and his eyes put out. The Assembly was hesitant. It was equally anxious about the intentions of the victorious general, but its members were afraid of popular reactions and eventually recommended a less conspicuous line of action: that Nicephorus should disappear, as though accidentally. The next day, therefore, he was brought to the Sacred Palace. Cedrenus has left us an interesting account of the subsequent interview, which shows that the outcome of events could never be predicted in Byzantium.

Nicephorus took the offensive from the start; his attitude was one of indignation and wounded surprise. He a conspirator! What a mockery, when the sole purpose of his visit to Byzantium was to hand in his resignation from the position of commander of the Eastern Army. And he produced his written resignation. To the astonished questioner he added that it was his intention to retire to a monastery, to prepare for salvation. 'Look!' he exclaimed as he dramatically uncovered his breast, as Phryne once did for other reasons; and there for all to see was a hard hair shirt.

Such a declaration, made in the right accents, might pass for the truth. Many were the Byzantines who, at the close of life, scorned vain successes in favour of true glory and retired into a monastery. Moreover, Nicephorus was known for his asceticism, his closest friend was a hermit and there was already a rumour that he was on the point of retiring to a monastery. The astounded Bringas was persuaded and, according to Cedrenus, he even fell to his knees to implore pardon. Nicephorus withdrew hastily and took refuge in St Sophia, the inviolable asylum of the persecuted.

Now Byzantium was a city of gossips, and it was useless to try to keep a secret there. A thousand sharp-eyed women and a hundred sharp-nosed men had soon ferreted out the news. A rumour flew from mouth to mouth, swelled, rumbled and burst. 'Yes, it is quite true, the last soldier of Christ, the saviour of the Empire, the idol of all is in danger of death. The only reward they have for him is assassination.' There were isolated shouts of protest, angry groups formed, men shook their fists and soon the surroundings of the great church were thronged with people. Nicephorus, judging the moment opportune, asked the Patriarch Polyeuctes to come to him. So here was a new personage, whose role in this drama was not small. He was a blundering and excitable old man. With Bible in hand he liked to thunder forth, like the prophets of old, a man of inspired wrath. The Greek people loved to listen to an angry prophet and were completely won over by him. Not without a certain delicious shudder they recalled his first official manifestation, about ten years before; on Easter Saturday, in the middle of the basilica, Constantine VII had received a sharp dressing down which, as Cedrenus tells us rather ingenuously, he did not appreciate. The poor Emperor was quite a gentle creature, but the Patriarch liked to startle his congregations, and had wanted to strike the keynote of his future addresses.

The strictness of his rule was all the more impressive because it followed a period of profligacy in his predecessor, Theophylact, who had been indeed a strange priest. Castrated at the age of sixteen by his father, he had quickly climbed all the stages of an ecclesiastical career, but this was no compensation to him for his loss of full manhood; this was to become most evident. For twenty years the devoted Byzantine Church resounded to an uninterrupted series of scandals and prevarications: bishops were consecrated in return for money, the most solemn offices were interrupted by profane dances, and religious ceremonial by pantomime.[1] He was passionately fond of horses and had 2,000 racers in his stables. They were fed on almonds, pistachios, raisins and figs, moistened with precious wine and perfumed with saffron or cinnamon. One day when his favourite mare was due to foal he was so nervous that he had to interrupt mass and return to the stables. He perished as he had sinned; returning with some young priests from a tempestuous ride along the Bosphorus coast, his stallion threw him against a wall and his skull was broken.

Polyeuctes hastened to Nicephorus. The venerable prelate was overcome at having been summoned by the powerful conqueror, the idol of the mob, whose virtue was renowned. He was delighted to take sides against that accursed prime minister who had cut him off from affairs for so long. Immediately he declared himself in favour of a radical solution. 'We must demand from the Senate the dismissal of Bringas!' Nicephorus tried to restrain him. It would suffice to demand the execution of the Imperial will, that is, his retention as commander of the Eastern Army. Polyeuctes did not understand and did not ask for an explanation; he even thought that Nicephorus had a Christian desire to forgive those who had offended him. But even more excited in support of the Cause, he hastened to the Regency Council,

---

[1] He introduced into the middle of the grave solemnities of the Greek Church, said Cedrenus, the inflexions of indecent voices, of laughter, of scandalous noise and songs borrowed from the street and the brothel.

where he made a moving intervention. 'How can you hesitate to confirm in office the conqueror of Crete, the victor of the Hamdanide? And this when we have a minor on the throne, a regency, a time of possible troubles! When Romanus II has formally demanded otherwise! What is the reason? Unworthy suspicions inspired by jealousy, personal ambitions and vanity!'

To mention the possibility of internal trouble and of palace revolution before an assembly of courtiers and the privileged is generally to ensure an attentive audience. Moreover the Senate

FIG. 49

Decoration from an eleventh-century manuscript

had just been badly shaken by the discovery of a conspiracy led by the former Emperor Stephen, one of the sons of Romanus Lecapenus. Stephen had been deposed by Constantine VII and exiled to Mytilene. But to foil his plot it had been necessary to poison him in the church of Methymna on Easter Saturday while he was taking communion. So Polyeuctes was not long in carrying the day. Not only was there now no question of putting out Nicephorus' eyes, but he was begged to resume his command, in the interests of public order in case of need. The general fear was so great that even Bringas was obliged to speak in favour of his mortal enemy.

Thus in a moment Nicephorus' situation had been completely transformed. Back in camp at Tzamandos he gradually regrouped his army; it was not Cilicia that he had in mind, nor the infidel, but, increasingly, Byzantium, Bringas, power....

It would be a mistake to think of Bringas as resigned. He had lost the first round but he was confident that he would win the second, and by the usual process: assassination. He was now seeking someone to do the job. To kill a general surrounded by his army was a difficult enterprise; probably a soldier would have more opportunities than other men. After having considered the points for and against certain individuals, he settled on a patrician who had formerly commanded the army in Italy, Marianos Argyros, also called Apambas. Yes, he might well agree: he was ambitious and reckless. He could be used today and eliminated tomorrow. Bringas made overtures. Would he be interested in appointment to a really high command—that of the Eastern Army, for example? And other things might go with it . . . the hand of the Empress Theophano, the last step before the supreme reward, the crown itself. Contrary to all expectations Argyros refused to take part. After all, few would be happy about taking on such an opponent. But he had a suggestion to make. Why not approach John Tzimisces, the cousin and brilliant second-in-command to Nicephorus? He was one of the most popular men in the Empire, and he was moreover in Tzamandos, on the spot!

This was sound advice. The one man whom the army might pardon for the murder of Nicephorus was Tzimisces. He is to play a significant part in the story, so the main facts about him must be given.

He was handsome, a detail which one day was to be important. Everyone praised his fresh complexion, his fiery hair, blue eyes, aquiline profile, his fine figure and square shoulders. In all athletic activities—archery, the rings, the javelin—he was outstanding, and no one could equal him in running and jumping. 'Like a bird on the wing,' wrote Leo the Deacon, 'he could fly over four horses standing abreast.' Of prodigious strength, with courage and audacity to match, 'he throws himself alone into a group of Saracen warriors, cuts them all down with his mighty sword and regains his own lines safe and sound'. He loved life and women and all good things. He was munificent, magnificent, generous to excess and delighted in pleasing all who asked anything of him. He was well-born, being a member of the great Armenian family of Courcouas, or Gourgen, which had supplied Byzantium with so many of her most valiant officers, of whom John Gourgen, who served Basil I, was without doubt the most famous; he was in addition endowed with the soundest military qualities. His only defect was a lack of height, but he made up for that by his extraordinary self-confidence.[1]

Without hesitation, Bringas took the advice; but for greater safety he also contacted Nicephorus' second lieutenant, who was also a kinsman of Tzimisces: Romanus Courcouas.

So it was that despatches were sent from the Sacred Palace to Tzamandos. 'Rid the Empire of your commander and you, Courcouas, will be made commander of the Army of the West; you, Tzimisces, will be made commander of the Eastern Army.' As the hand of Theophano seemed to go with the eastern command Tzimisces also saw himself as her husband.

When the two men received these messages, Nicephorus, who was unwell, was asleep. Without hesitating they immediately rushed into his tent and shook him violently.

'You sleep,' cried Tzimisces, 'while a miserable eunuch is plotting your downfall! Read this!' And he handed him the message.

'What shall I do?' asked Nicephorus with a false show of despair.

'What shall you do! Put on the Imperial diadem and set out for Constantinople!'

Nicephorus put up a show of resistance, but the others threatened him with their swords. Suddenly he dropped his pretence. He stood up, turned towards Byzantium and swore to lead them to victory.

* * *

At dawn on July 3, 963, the entire Eastern Army was assembled outside the walls of Caesarea, the capital of Cappadocia.

With their swords in their hands, the corps commanders emerged from their tents and, led by John Tzimisces, they moved towards the general's pavilion. They asked to be received and Nicephorus appeared. The swords suddenly shot forward and each man cried 'Greetings, Autocrator of the Romans! All powerful Basileus, long may you reign! Long may you live!'

At these words strategoi, counts and turmarchs ran forward in

[1] It has been suggested that Tzimisces is a corruption of the Armenian Tchemeschguig, a nickname given to short people.

their thousands with the same cry. 'Long life to Nicephorus the August One! Long life to the Invincible Emperor whom God protects! Forward to Byzantium!' Nicephorus was lifted from the ground and hoisted on to a great shield, in the ancient manner.

He protested and spoke humbly of himself. He was no politician—why invest him with power? Moreover, the world weighed heavily upon him. He had found no solace in it since the death of his wife and his only son, and his desire was to withdraw into the religious life. Why not choose Tzimisces? Gradually, as though reluctantly, he bowed to the general will,

FIG. 50
Christ as King. Upper part of a triptych in the Vatican Museum

and on his feet the *campagia* were placed, those famous purple shoes, embroidered with golden eagles, which as a symbol of the supreme power were reserved for the Basileus. But he made a clever move when offered the *stemma* and the check-patterned robe. Not yet! He had no wish, he said, to dethrone the little *porphyrogenetes* (the princes); he would simply replace the infamous Bringas as their protector.

Thus Nicephorus was Autocrator by virtue of a military revolution. To thank his faithful army, he ascended a hillock according to custom, and from there, surrounded by his officers, with lance in hand and sword in belt, he spoke to his men assembled around him under the blue sky. 'Soldiers! I am Basileus at your request. We can no longer tolerate the government of this miserable eunuch. I shall be faithful to you until death. Be you likewise faithful to me. Alas, Roman blood will probably be shed, for it is not the Arabs of Crete or Syria that we shall have to fight, but Roman soldiers. We shall have to take the very capital of this mighty Empire, and it will not be captured like a simple Saracen *kastron*. The effort will be great and painful. But God will be on our side, for Bringas has cruelly offended Him. Put your trust in me. Follow me. I will lead you to victory.'

This half-religious, half-military speech was greeted with enthusiastic cheers. Every man declared himself willing to die for Phocas. But Christ's help too must be enrolled, so Phocas and his senior officers hastened to the cathedral to ask for the blessing of the Metropolitan.

Now Nicephorus really felt himself to be Emperor and without waiting to be acclaimed by the people and the Senate he began to act like a sovereign, making appointments and dismissals. He despatched messengers in all directions. His most trustworthy officers galloped towards the Black Sea and the Straits, holding under their cloaks their commissions as theme and fortress commanders; the important points on the coast would be secure before Bringas knew what was happening.

Tzimisces was, of course, well rewarded. He received the rank of *Magistros*—the highest Palace official—and succeeded Nicephorus at the head of the Eastern Army, the highest command in the Empire.

It was important to act quickly. Leaving his deputy to hold the frontier, the usurper made his way by forced marches to the capital. He had sent on before him Philotus, Bishop of Euchaita, with letters for the Patriarch, the *parakimomenus* and the Senate. They bore the following message. 'I am your Basileus and the guardian of the Autocrators until they come of age. I shall arrive without delay at Constantinople. Receive me as your master in all things and I will preserve your dignities and grant you new ones. If not, you will perish by fire and sword.'

*   *   *

Poor Philotus was badly received in Constantinople, for on him fell Bringas' stupefied fury. Loaded with chains, flung into prison, he was treated 'like the envoy of some Scythian sovereign, some miserable Barbarian chief'.

The eunuch's disillusion was great. So this was how his plans had worked out! Right, he would take up the challenge. He had troops. The Macedonian battalions were at that moment in barracks in Byzantium, so they could work off some of their hatred of the Armenians.[1] Nor was there any dearth of military commanders; Marianos Apambas, Paschal, Nicholas and Leon Tornice[2] would all be very pleased to crush Nicephorus. The walls were sound. He personally was confident of his own ability and power to strengthen resistance. Immediately the strategic points were occupied, the walls were sealed and the harbour blocked. Constantinople was now a closed town, squatting behind a thousand look-out slits and three hundred towers. Let the rebel come!

Finally, on August 9 he was seen on the opposite shore of the Bosphorus, at Chrysopolis, today called Scutari. The decisive moment was near.

Bringas at once made sure of his rear by laying hands on the relations and friends of Nicephorus. There was no doubt about their fate—today prison, tomorrow torture—eyes put out, hands cut off, tongues torn out. In this round-up, his enemy's father, Bardas Phocas, fell into his hands.

The people were in a fever of excitement; crowds formed in the street and there was excited speculation. 'If it was not for these Macedonians, Bringas' account would soon be settled!' At first the revolt was vague and shapeless, but there was at least one man eager to give it point and direction: the eunuch Basil, the celebrated bastard of the Emperor Lecapenus. He hated the First Minister who had taken from him the office of *parakimomenus*. Covered with honours by Constantine VII and stripped of them by Romanus II, he longed to become again First Chamberlain and leader of the Senate. He was in fact a strange man and he had rapidly climbed the administrative ladder. A few months after having been made a patrician he was appointed

---

[1] Nicephorus' troops were mostly Armenians.
[2] Although the Tornices were Armenians they hated the Phocas family.

commander of the Grand Hetairia, the most famous corps of the guard, composed of Russians and Scandinavian Vaerangians. Soon he was First Chamberlain and leader of the Senate. He even rose to the rank of general and in 958 gained a striking victory over the Saracens for which he was honoured in the Circus. He was resolute, energetic and adventurous; he had all the qualities of a leader of men.

However, it was the octogenarian Bardas Phocas who put the spark to the powder. In spite of his age he had escaped from his guards and taken refuge in St Sophia. The servants of the law who had been pursuing him called to him to come out. He refused and shouted for help. The people loved this veteran of the Asian wars and he was quickly joined by sympathizers, many of them armed. Soon his supporters had overrun the Great Church and chased the eunuch's agents from it. Henceforth the old *magistros* was under the protection of the people, who showed their anger, when patrician friends of Bringas tried to snatch him away, and caused them to flee.

On hearing the news the Prime Minister went to the spot. Reaching St Sophia, he dismounted in the midst of a hostile crowd. He went in to see the Patriarch[1] and formally demanded the escaped prisoner. Polyeuctes refused.

Increasingly irritated, he went back surrounded by his guards. The crowd was still there and he was greeted by jeers and catcalls. But he began to speak. Was he hoping to win people over? It would be difficult to say, for cold and haughty as he was he did not know how to appease or persuade. A veritable diatribe escaped his lips. 'Enough of this shouting! Move away from the church at once or you will pay dearly!' 'He was haughty, abusive and atrocious beyond words,' wrote a chronicler. Over the clamour he repeated mechanically, 'I will treat you in such a way, I will punish you so harshly, I will starve you so thoroughly, that you will die! I will make you pay a golden coin for so little wheat that you can hold it in the fold of your cloaks!'

Putting his threat into execution straight away he went to the Golden Milestone to stop the sale of bread. The morning wore

[1] The Patriarcheion, the residence of the Patriarch, adjoined the Church and looked on to the Augusteon.

on and at midday people began to go home to eat; the area round the church emptied. This was the moment for which Bringas had been waiting. Taking the little basileis he hastened to St Sophia. This time he avoided the public square by using the arcade which connected the Sacred Palace and St Sophia. Bardas Phocas was almost alone and the Prime Minister miraculously produced soothing words. 'What are you afraid of, my friend? Why do you resist? I do not wish you any harm. Follow me and you will be protected.' Weakened by age and the emotions of the day, the octogenarian allowed himself to be led away. At the hour of vespers the great church refilled. The crowd could not find its protégé and in a flash its anger exploded. It was clear that he had been betrayed by the clergy and without any further explanation being sought the Patriarch was injured and some priests were stoned.

Thoroughly alarmed, Polyeuctes went to the Sacred Palace as quickly as he could, gave an account of what had happened and persuaded Bringas to release the hostage. He reappeared outside St Sophia holding Bardas by the hand; the crowd calmed down. But messengers appeared with an order: 'The old *magistros* must not return to St Sophia.' Then he was not safe! The people rose. The disturbance became a revolution. People surrounded Bardas and led him to his home. Others seized pieces of wood, bricks, railings, rushed to the Forum and set upon the Macedonian soldiers. At this moment the eunuch Basil appeared, followed by his 3,000 armed retainers.[1] Acclaimed, he assumed leadership of the movement. It spread like a powder-trail from street to street and quarter to quarter, so that the whole town was soon alight. The regular troops were better equipped but the revolutionaries were more numerous. A thousand took the place of every hundred who were killed. There were so many bodies on the marble pavements that movement was difficult. Harassed and submerged, the battalions lost their cohesion, gradually separated and finally broke into fragments. With great shouts of joy the population mopped them up one after the other. The smallest incidents favoured the rebels. From the top of a house an old woman threw a chamber pot at a galloping horseman and knocked him out flat. It was Apambas, the centre

[1] This figure sheds some light on the mode of life of a high Byzantine official.

of resistance. Basil could now proclaim Nicephorus at every crossroad. The eunuch had definitely lost the game.

And now for three days and nights the city was the prey of rioters. No one was spared, neither rich nor poor. Many grim acts of revenge were perpetrated in badly lit side streets.

Finally, memories were restored. Nicephorus, the cause of the rising, was still there, immobilized across the Bosphorus. He must be brought in. Quickly people rushed to the walls and broke open the gates. Nicephorus was summoned from one shore to the other. People were shouting 'Long live Nicephorus the August! Long live Nicephorus the Ever Victorious!' The old senators were as excited as anyone else.

The Golden Horn was soon taken by assault. The vessels of the fleet—*ousia, pamphilia, triremes, dromons*—were overrun, unmoored and pushed out to sea. Finally they reached him and everyone thrust himself as near to the new Emperor as possible, anxious to look at him and acclaim him.

But Nicephorus was to stay several more days at Chrysopolis, in order to work out with the great officials the principal modalities of his rule. On the 14th his brother, Leo Phocas, crossed the Straits with a vanguard and took possession of the capital in his name. The last interviews took place on the 15th. Basil the Bastard was once again Great Chamberlain, and another Basil, *prepositor*, and a few other high officials had been summoned. They spent the night with the Basileus; the next day they would take part in the triumphal entry.

According to custom, on the eve of this great day, the Basileus of the Romans had to address a letter to the Patriarch, couched in conventional terms: 'I believe in one God, an all-powerful Father who has made sky, earth. . . .[1] In addition I confirm, confess and approve of the apostolic and inspired decisions and the constitutions and definitions of the seven oecumenical councils and of the local councils and the privileges and customs of the Most Holy Church of God. I confirm and approve of all that the Holy Fathers have established and defined legally and canonically. In addition I promise to remain always the true and faithful slave and son of the Most Holy Church and to be its defender and avenger, to be clement and philanthropic towards

---

[1] Here followed the rest of the Creed.

my subjects as far as justice and the proprieties will permit and to abstain from killings and mutilations as much as possible and to pursue truth and justice. I repudiate and anathematize all that the Holy Fathers have repudiated and anathematized and with all my soul, with all my heart and with all my mind I believe in the Creed which I have written in this letter and I intend in the Holy and Apostolic Catholic Church of God to maintain these things. Written on the fifteenth day of the month of August. I, Nicephorus, faithful Emperor of Christ and Basileus of the Romans have written and signed with my own hand all that precedes and I place it in the hands of my Most Holy Lord the Oecumenical Patriarch Polyeuctes and the divine and Most Holy Synod.'

FIG. 51

Various renderings of the Chrisma in the Byzantine Empire

* * *

Could anything equal in munificence the coronation of the Basileus? Its most outstanding features were the violence of the colours, the splendour of the ritual and the crowd's delirium. The Byzantines had a genius for this kind of spectacle; both contemplative and sensual, they expressed themselves in striking contrasts. Doubtless their fetes were of spiritual origin; but they had a pagan *éclat*.

Nicephorus had passed in prayer the night of August 15 to 16. The sun was about to rise. A great day was beginning.

Gently moving on the blue waters of the Bosphorus, the Imperial *dromon* awaited with all oars showing, like some fabulous monster with a hundred golden tongues. It was decked in ceremonial array. At the stern and along the sides, the sphinxes, the lions and the sirens stood out from a background of streaming banners. At the prow a statue of St George stood out, striking in its whiteness, against crimson standards. On the centre of the deck, under a circle of garlands, was the purple pavilion, borne upon gilded caryabides, which contained the silver throne. At dawn the new Basileus entered it and gave the signal to depart. Escorted by the fleet, the galley soon moved off. It quickly crossed the Bosphorus, moved along the coastal wall of Byzantium and reached the port of Theodosius, touching land near the monastery of the Abramites.[1]

Nicephorus stepped ashore and, followed by the highest officials, came to the Magnaura Palace. From here he would set out at the head of his troops for the great triumphal march of six miles. He now wore golden armour. His horse had a shining breastplate, its flanks were covered with purple cloth and its head with precious stones.

Preceded by six flamoula[2] of precious materials and bearing a sword in his hand he first crossed the Kampos, the great military parade ground. He dismounted in front of the Church of St John Hebdomon; inside he said a prayer and lit candles. His metamorphosis had begun; for he must change gradually from the victorious general to the representative of Christ on earth. He emerged from the church with the crossed sceptre in his hand and dressed in the *sagion* of hyacinth purple and the *scaramangion* of precious furs.

The entire route of the procession was lined with people: the famous and the humble, rich and poor, noblemen, militiamen of the Factions, townsmen, innumerable monks, artisans in thousands, Thracian and Bithynian peasants, soldiers and sailors on leave. In spite of the blazing sun and torrid heat, people held up lighted torches, burned incense and waved flags. Trumpets, horns, drum and cymbals gave out their discordant and raucous notes. Everybody shouted, yelled and applauded. With great difficulty the procession forced a way along the road of great stone slabs, and at last reached the Great Wall of the Golden Gate.

Nicephorus dismounted and three times prostrated himself towards the East. Then, bedecked with roses, myrtle and rosemary by hundreds of children, he rode under the central and highest arch.

[1] Also known as the Monastery of the Virgin of Achiropoietos—'that which was not made by the hand of man'. The monastery contained one of the most celebrated of the so-called miraculous images of the Mother of Christ, which were so venerated in the East.

[2] Brightly coloured pennons.

There was silence. Then with a hundred different formulae, and in an order strictly laid down, the Factions began to chant their official ovations, to proclaim in strange rhythm the merits of their new master. 'Welcome, Nicephorus, Basileus of the Romans! Welcome, great prince, who have put Hagar's armies[1] to flight and destroyed their cities. Welcome, Great Victor! Welcome, August One! You have subdued the barbarians. From you, on bended knee did Ishmael beg for mercy. By you has the sway of the Roman people been increased. May your reign be strong and prosperous! God had pity on his people, Nicephorus, when he made you Basileus and Autocrator of the Romans. Rejoice then, city of the Romans! Welcome with transports of joy Nicephorus crowned by God, who comes to light up by his splendour the whole surface of the inhabitable earth!'

All this time the Basileus sat on a motionless horse, with his head held high, erect and proud, and deigned to listen to his praises. Eventually, the procession began to move again, and soon arrived in the centre of the town and made its way down the Mese, Byzantium's most famous avenue.

FIG. 52

Sixth century Bishop (after Hottenroth)

Palaces and houses were almost hidden behind garlands and decorations. Everything was bedecked for the occasion—triumphal arches, the public squares, obelisks. And in the blinding light, the heads of silver statues, surmounted on wreathed columns, shone like pearls.

Finally they reached the Augusteon. Once again the procession halted. Nicephorus dismounted and entered the little church of the Most Holy Theotokos, Mother of God. In the sanctuary he knelt and, candles in hand, worshipped the miraculous icon. There, his metamorphosis was completed. He emerged as the

[1] A reference to the Saracens.

image of Christ himself, dressed in *debetesion*, the long narrow tunic with wide sleeves which fell to the heels, crowned with the white tiara and wearing the purple *campagia*. He crossed the Augusteon, passed under the Arch of the Golden Milestone[1] and, followed by the crowd, walked towards St Sophia.

From the steps which went round the square a senator threw out thousands of pieces of bread, each containing three golden coins, three silver coins and three copper coins, an act which commemorated the ancient bounty of the consuls. At the porch of his church, surrounded by its vast staff of priests, stood the Patriarch, holding out the Holy Cross.

Suddenly Nicephorus was hoisted up on to a shield, presented to the crowd and acclaimed.

He was now confirmed in his position by the people and could cross the threshold of the Holy Church. In the Horologion room—which got its name from the sundial it contained—the Factions resumed their eulogies. Let an extract from them suffice. 'The public welfare demands Nicephorus as Emperor. The court, the army, the people, the Senate ask for him in their prayers. The world expects him. For the common good let Nicephorus reign! Grant our wish, oh God! Long life to Nicephorus! Nicephorus the August, only thou art pious, only thou art August! God has given thee to us. May God protect thee! Live for ever as soldier and servant of Christ! May Nicephorus reign through the ages! Oh God, protect your most Christian Empire!'

FIG. 53

Sixth century priest (after Hottenroth)

Then, accompanied by the Patriarch, Nicephorus crossed the Room of the Holy Well. Again he divested himself, this time in the Metatorion, passed through the great door of the Basilike

---

[1] From this point all distances were measured in Byzantium.

and mounted the *ambon*.[1] The crown, the *chlamys* and other imperial emblems were set out on a portable altar; the Patriarch blessed them. Now, aided by attendants, the Basileus dressed himself, and while doing so recited sometimes in a low voice, sometimes in a loud voice the prayers prescribed by usage.

The solemn moment was at hand. The Emperor leaned forward and put his hands together. The crowd stopped breathing. The Grand Pontiff approached him, chanting, took off his tiara,

FIG. 54

The Three Wise Men, from a sixth century mosaic in St Apollinare, Ravenna

anointed him with the sign of the cross, and finally placed the diadem on his head. Great chords of music from the organs suddenly filled the church. Polyeuctes intoned the famous Hymn to the Trinity and three times priests, senators, Factions and people repeated it. 'Holy, Holy, Holy! Glory to God in the Highest and on earth peace to all men. Long live Nicephorus, Great Basileus and Autocrator!'

But Ecclesiasticus has said that all is vanity here below, and amidst the splendours of the coronation the new Basileus must

[1] This was a throne of stone veined with gold. Justinian had paid a fabulous price for it: an amount equal to a year's tribute from Egypt.

remember that. So the Patriarch handed him the *akakia*, a small silken bag containing ashes of the dead.

The Emperor acknowledged it and left a number of golden coins on the altar. Then, escorted by a hundred Varangians bearing battle-axes, and a hundred armed young nobles, he descended from the *ambon* by the opposite side. He crossed the church and sat upon a throne on a platform of porphyry. The adoration was about to begin.

FIG. 55

The Adoration of the Magi, from the sarcophagus of the Exarch Isaac, at Ravenna

Presenting themselves by rank, or *vela*, the high officials prostrated themselves and then devoutly embraced his knees— *magistros*, patricians, *strategoï*, *protospatharies*, commanders of the guard, senators, *hypatoï*, *spatharies*, *stratores*, *kometes* of the *scholae*, *scribones*, *protosecretis*, *vestitores*, *silentiaries*, *mandatores*, etc., etc.

At the 'If you please' of the presiding Grand Eunuch, each one wished the Basileus long life, and answering them with 'May you be happy', like a marionette, he turned and walked away. Now was Nicephorus in truth Autocrator of the Romans, isapostole—'that is to say, the equal of the apostles, successor of the most pious Constantine, the representative of divine power on earth.'

And so another *coup d'état* had succeeded. Would the new regime last? It had every appearance of permanency. Supported by the army and the people and endowed with exceptional military ability, the Emperor might reasonably expect many years of happiness. But let us move forward six years and see. . . .

* * *

The night of December 10, 969, was dark and there was no moon. Curious figures, disguised as women, furtively entered the Imperial gynaeceum. Arms were concealed under their robes. Without difficulty they passed through dark rooms and finally arrived in the boudoir of the Empress, the still radiant Theophano, now the wife of Nicephorus. With a finger to her lips she ordered them to be quiet. As though he had a presentiment of evil the Basileus had caused his wife's apartments to be searched from top to bottom on several occasions recently, but the Officer of the Cubiculum, the chief of the eunuchs and the master of the household had found nothing. With noiseless tread the Basilissa led them towards a little recess just outside the Emperor's room. At the right moment they would only have to leap from their hiding place. . . . Then, still without speaking, she went to her husband. Would he deign tonight to have her in his bed? Nicephorus had never been able to say no to Theophano, even now when he no longer desired her. She thanked him with a kiss. Then she suddenly remembered that she had to see some young Bulgarian princesses who were visiting the Palace. 'I shall soon come back,' she said. 'Wait for me, and be sure not to lock your door.' Nicephorus agreed and became absorbed in his prayers. Minutes went by, till at last, overcome by fatigue, he wrapped himself up in the old hair shirt that had belonged to his uncle, St Maleinos, and fell asleep. Images of Christ, the Theotokos and the Evangelist watched over him . . . but the door remained open.

However, the leader of the plot had not yet arrived; he was John Tzimisces who, a year ago, had become the Empress's lover. The *gnomon* had just announced the time: five o'clock in the morning. Outside it was intensely cold and snow was falling heavily. A strong wind whipped up the Propontis. The conspirators were anxiously staring out to sea. One of them had even posted himself outside on an open terrace of the Imperial *kastron*, with his sword in his hand. But he saw nothing, and he heard nothing but the noise of wind and sea. Then suddenly a small craft appeared, buffeted about by the sea. There were four men on board—Tzimisces and three companions. The skiff landed behind the Bucoleon Palace, near a group in marble representing a fight between a bull and a lion. A light whistle, the agreed signal, was heard. And now willow baskets appeared through the windows and were slowly lowered on the end of ropes. The four men got in and were pulled up to the room where Theophano and the others were anxiously waiting.

As soon as they were together they drew their swords and Theophano led them into the Imperial bedroom—the door was still unlocked. A dreadful surprise awaited them—the bed was empty! The Emperor had heard of the plot! They were lost! Some of them at once prepared to dive into the sea from the top of the ramparts, when a little eunuch appeared and signalled them to be quiet. He pointed to a corner of the room and there on a hard litter was a sleeping figure. It was the Basileus! Then they all, like beasts of prey, rushed upon him and kicked him awake. The Autocrator raised himself up on an elbow. Without hesitation one of them split his head with a terrible blow from his sword. With forehead and eyebrow cut to the bone and his cheek sliced, Nicephorus cried in anguish, 'Theotokos, help me!' He was blinded by blood but they dragged him to the foot of the great bed where Tzimesces was sitting. Regardless of his terrible wound they ordered him to kneel, but he could not hold himself upright and fell to the ground. Tzimisces heaped invective upon him and the conspirators joined in, their hatred released. 'Answer me, you miserable tyrant,' cried Tzimisces. 'Was it not due to me that you came to the throne, that you became an all-powerful Emperor? Forgetful of all my benefits, blinded by the deepest envy, you disgraced me, took from me my army command and exiled me to the country with peasants and oafs, I, whom everyone loves and respects, as you are hated by all. But now you are in my power! None will take you from me! All the same, if you have anything to say for yourself, speak! I am listening.'

What could Nicephorus reply? Instead, in a loud voice, he continued to invoke the help of God and the Theotokos.

Then they set upon him. One knocked his teeth out with his sword handle. Another pulled tufts out of his beard. Then someone smashed his jaw. Finally, Tzimisces dealt him full in the face a blow which split his skull. After that the others were striking a dead body. Meanwhile Theophano was listening to this nightmare scene from behind the door.

All this had made a great noise which had rudely awakened the Palace. Servants came running up from all sides. Outside the

FIG. 56

Detail from an ivory chest at Sens

guards were rushing forward with axes to try to force the bronze doors. Then there was a furious fight. The conspirators were getting the worst of it when one of them, with a sudden inspiration, cut off the dead man's head and brandished it through the window in the light of torches. In the snowstorm, 30 feet from the ground, the only bright spot is the Emperor's head, the long hair dripping with blood. Seeing it, the mercenaries suddenly stopped. Now that all was lost and their master was dead, why go on? There was nothing to do but take orders from his successor.

What of the people who had so ardently protested their love for Nicephorus and had raised him to the throne? They came the next day to stare with shudders of delight at his decapitated body, bloodstained and unrecognizable in the snow. Not a single man rose to protest, not a regret marred the concerted acclamations. The wheel still turned, and the history of Byzantium continued upon its course . . . and ten years later it was the turn of John Tzimisces to die at the hand of an assassin.

BYZANTIUM
AND
THE
WEST

For the Byzantine the Roman Empire had never ceased to exist. The fall of Rome in the fifth century did not mean that it was decapitated, but simply that it was no longer two-headed. It still survived, as glorious as ever, along the shores of the Bosphorus, centred on Constantinople, the new *Urbs*. To make the illusion more complete, the Byzantines, who spoke and read only Greek, and whose dress, homes and manners had nothing Latin about them, proudly continued to call themselves

FIG. 57

*Scene from Genesis in St Mark's, Venice, thirteenth century
The creation of birds and fishes*

Romans. This concept was bound to have profound repercussions in Imperial politics. If Rome survived in Constantinople, all the lands which the barbarians held in the west were nothing less than irredeemed provinces whose sovereignty Byzantium had inherited; indeed, the occupation of Italy by the Germans had long been for her like that of Alsace-Lorraine for France. If there was no Holy Roman Empire except the Byzantine, then the German one could only be a harmful and presumptuous masquerade. Similarly, the Pope had no right to the pre-eminence which he claimed; he was nothing more than a simple bishop, that of the new Rome. He was, moreover, a bishop in whom Constantinople had no confidence, for he had dared to propose and to accept changes in dogma which were not recognized by the Orthodox Church.

Briefly, relations between Byzantium and the West rested upon explosive foundations which led to a number of wars, or at least to a state of cold war.

Two events—the one much more important than the other—illustrate the relationship. One was the Byzantine venture in Italy and the other the extraordinary mission on which Otto II sent Bishop Liudprand to the court in Constantinople.

'The Greater Greece'

The first great clash between the Germanic and the Byzantine worlds came a century after the fall of Rome and it naturally occurred in Italy.

During the fifth century the whole peninsula had been overrun by the barbarians. Cassiodorus, the champion of the crumbling Latin world, faced a grave dilemma of a kind familiar in our own day: should he call on Byzantium for help; should he, that is, seek the protection of an overseas power possessed of a strong navy, or should he come to terms with the conqueror of the moment, who was invincible on land? Briefly, should he resist or collaborate? He chose to collaborate. Right through the fifth century and the first decades of the sixth century, Italy lay in the hands of the conquerors: conquerors who were soon conquered by a softness of living and a culture superior to their own.

But early in the sixth century in Byzantium the reign of Justinian began, and although he has enjoyed a well merited fame in the law schools as the formulator of a legal code, it was above all as a military commander that he was appreciated in the Eastern Empire. Under his impulse Byzantium found itself possessed at last of the means required by its political philosophy. The first task to which it turned was the re-conquest of the lost Roman provinces. So in the year 535 a Byzantine army embarked for Italy and after 27 years the peninsula was freed. Italy was 'Roman' again; that is to say the country was covered by a centralized Byzantine administration and the Pope recognized the supremacy of Constantinople. In exchange the Greeks acknowledged the supremacy of the Pope in the West, with the result that from the Alps to the Straits of Messina the Church—the rallying force—remained one, Catholic and Latin.

As earlier developments foreshadowed, this political marriage did not and could not last. If the Catholic and Latin West was going to be under the administrative and religious control of the Greek and Orthodox East, either it would have to be Hellenized or it would have to be given a large measure of local autonomy. An Empire which declared itself to be universal was going to find it difficult to follow the latter alternative, above all at a time of religious strife. So when Byzantium adopted iconoclasm in the eighth century, she tried to enforce the destruction of all images and icons, 'these remnants of fetishism', in Italy as elsewhere, and risings ensued. Rome evicted its governor and gave temporal authority to Pope Gregory II. The citizens of Ravenna killed their exarch and placed themselves under the Lombard King Liudprand. The Duke of Naples was assassinated. Soon the whole of Northern and Central Italy was lost and Southern Italy—Calabria, Apulia and Otranto—was going that way. In this situation the government in Constantinople resorted to extreme measures. Rather than give up the last provinces which remained in the West of the Roman heritage, it was decided that they should be completely Hellenized. Thus, if Calabria, Apulia and Otranto lost their Latin culture and for three centuries, until the Norman conquest, were entirely Greek in speech, culture and religion, it was because Byzantium liked to think that Rome survived in herself.

It is one of the great ironies of history that the instruments of this policy of assimilation were none other than those thousands of Greek iconodules, both monks and laymen, who had fled from

Byzantium and sought in Southern Italy refuge from persecution. The iconoclast Emperor Leo the Isaurian ordered his officials in Italy to leave them entirely free to worship their images and even to ensure for each one a peaceful asylum. And these refugees spent themselves without counting the cost. Through-

FIG. 58

Cover of a reliquary at Limbourg, made on the orders of Emperors Constantine and Romanus between 949 and 959; enamel

out the land they ministered to the unfortunate and edified the faithful by the example of their virtue. There were many factors in their favour: they were numerous; they had the prestige of orthodoxy; their background was a higher, richer and more stimulating civilization. At a time when by comparison life in

PLATE 12.
The ambo of St Mark's, Venice

The Byzantine ambo of Salerno Cathedral

PLATE 13.
The dome of the Baptistry, St Mark's, Venice

Monreale Cathedral

the Latin West was obscure and barbaric, their monasteries were remarkable for the vigour of their theology and philosophy. The whole peninsula, and later the whole of Europe eagerly snatched at the 'Lives of the Saints' and other manuscripts they produced. Gradually the country surrendered itself: in a comparatively short time, only the Greek language was to be heard, and in churches Orthodox rites replaced the Catholic. Byzantine towns like Tarentum, Catazaron (present-day Catanzaro) and Miletus grew up. New constructions appeared, such as the bridge of the seven arches at Tarentum and the aqueduct nearly 25 miles long which brought the lovely waters of the Vallenza down from the mountains. Eastern reliquaries found their way into the churches; many of them are still to be found in towns like Otranto, Barcetta, Amalfi, Salerno, Messina and Palermo. They all had their legend, but none could compare with that attaching to the Virgin of Hodigitria which was, perhaps, the most famous image in Byzantium. It

FIG. 59

Sarcophagus at Ravenna (sculptured stone)

had a supernatural power and had many times dispersed invading armies and fleets of Avars, Saracens, Bulgars and Persians. On such occasions, while melodious hymns and canticles were sung, it was accorded triumphal honours and escorted through the Golden Gate; it was, indeed, the palladium of the city. Leo the Isaurian, the iconoclast Emperor, condemned it, along with all the others. But we learn from the Synaxorion of the Greek Church at Bari, which was written in the tenth or eleventh century by the priest Glegoris, that two monks resolved to save it. They locked it in a chest and shipped it secretly on board one of the galleys which took part in the punitive expedition against Pope Gregory II. Consequently it went to sea in January 733. In the Adriatic a great storm arose which scattered the ships, destroying some of them. But the Virgin of Hodigitria was saved. The chronicle explains what happened: '. . . there descended from the sky an angel in the form of a young man of the greatest beauty who gave heart to the terrified crew of the vessel in which this miraculous Virgin was hidden and, seizing the helm, conducted the boat safe and sound into the port of Bari, the first Tuesday of the month of March.'

It is understandable that, faced with this unique work of conquest and total assimilation, some historians have been able to say: 'The story of the Western monks has been set down with much eloquence; the story of the Eastern monks, no less glorious, is still to be written. There is no doubt that one of its finest chapters will be that which tells of the eighth-century exodus to Calabria and the conquest of this country lapsed almost into barbarism for the Greek culture; a conquest which was made by men rejected as unworthy by their own misguided homeland. The children of St Basil were the worthy successors, in their civilizing work, of St Benedict.'[1]

The Mission of My Lord Liudprand

The extraordinary mission with which the German Emperor Otto II had charged Liudprand, Bishop of Cremona, was the negotiation of a marriage. He hoped that his son would marry a Byzantine princess, who would bring as her dowry nothing other than Greater Greece itself.

The principal interest of the story of this mission, apart from its picturesque qualities, is to be found in the light it sheds on

[1] F. Lenormant, *La Grande Grèce*.

the contempt mixed with indignation which the Eastern Empire felt for the Western German Holy Roman Empire, an attitude which resulted from Byzantium's cherished belief that she was the sole inheritor of the Roman Empire.

The Bishop Liudprand was not unknown in Constantinople, where he had stayed 20 years previously, and he liked to think that he still had many friends there. So he was full of optimism concerning the outcome of his mission when, on Thursday, June 4, 968, he set out for 'the God-protected town'. The arrival of an ambassador was usually an important event in Byzantium: the Factions lined the streets in their ceremonial costumes, the Golden Gate was re-covered with gold and garlands and the Mese was decorated. On behalf of the Basileus high officials in ceremonial brocade costumes went down to the quay to welcome the distinguished guest. But how different it was on this occasion! The Golden Gate stood naked and all was silent and deserted: no Factions, no garlands, no officials. Only customs officials, and they barred the way for Liudprand and his suite when they made to enter through the Golden Gate. An order had in fact been made provisionally forbidding him from entering the town. Why? It was not known; it was just an order. For several hours in torrential rain the ambassador of the Germanic Holy Roman Emperor paced up and down outside the walls. At last messengers appeared bearing the permit he had been waiting for. Quickly he mounted a horse, but when he made to enter the city two officials rushed towards him, threw him off his mount and took possession of it. Why? It was not known; it was just an order. So he was obliged to walk to the palace, the Marble Palace it was called, which the government had placed at his disposal. After walking several hours through dirty and malodorous streets he arrived at his destination. The 'Marble Palace' turned out to be a broken-down stone building which did not keep out the rain. Inside, the walls were wet and the furniture was covered with mildew. In the days which followed the ambassador was to have only too many opportunities to find that the board in no way made up for the lodging. The food was badly cooked and for drink there was only Byzantine wine, whose acidity gave him hiccups and stomach pains, for he was dyspeptic. In order to get water he had to buy it at a ruinous price from water-sellers in the street. The housekeeper, 'in reality a spy', he noted in his journal, charged a high commission on the smallest purchase and cheated him whenever possible. 'Ah, you would have to search hell,' wrote Liudprand more than once, 'to find as great a rascal as this!'

Badly lodged and badly fed, the ambassador was also cut off from the outside world. No news reached him from court. Whenever he wanted to go out or receive visitors, sentinels with sword in hand blocked the threshold under the pretext of ensuring his safety. More than a week passed in this way. At last, on the Saturday before Whitsuntide a message arrived saying that he was expected at the Sacred Palace at once. Liudprand hastily got ready. But he searched in vain for horse or litter and was forced to set out on foot. On that particular day the streets were almost impassable, for during the whole of the previous night such a storm had raged that large numbers of people had hastened to church to ask God for his clemency, so certain were they that the end of the world was at hand. Even on normal days no person of rank ventured into the city without a vehicle, so dirty and noisome were the streets; but today it was very much worse. Down the public buildings fell ceaseless cascades of water. Private houses with broken roofs were spilling forth the night's rain. In the lanes rushing torrents carried away man and beast. There were holes and quagmires everywhere—and it was several miles from the Marble Palace to the Sacred Palace!

It is difficult to believe that the court had not deliberately summoned him on this day. More than once in the course of the journey, with cassock held high, the bishop had to jump, and more than once, misjudging the distance, he had landed in a muddy pool. After an hour and a half of acrobatic progress he arrived at his destination, only to find the doors of the Sacred Palace closed to him. The doorkeeper or *papias* pretended that he had not received instructions about him and only after much discussion was Otto's ambassador admitted.

The Basileus Nicephorus Phocas did not deign to appear and his brother the *curopalate* Leo was deputizing for him. On seeing this muddy prelate, Leo gave free rein to his hilarity. After a few acidly polite remarks had been exchanged they came to the crucial point.

'In your meeting tomorrow with the Basileus,' inquired Leo, 'how will you refer to your master?'

'By his title of Emperor, of course,' replied Liudprand.

Upon hearing these words the fury of the Byzantine burst forth: 'There is only one Emperor in the world!' he cried. 'And he lives in the Sacred Palace. At the most, your master is a king, one of the many barbarian princes whom we honour by deigning to receive their representatives.'

Having said this, he got up and went. The interview was over. We may guess at Liudprand's indignation. That evening he poured out all his bile on to a piece of parchment: 'Leo is no more than a knave, a cur that would bite the hand that fed it.' The ceremony on the morrow did not open with much promise of success.

It was Sunday, June 7, the day of Pentecost. The Basileus sat on his famous golden throne in the Triclinium, at the top of several steps, motionless and expressionless, in accordance with tradition. He was attended by all the members of the Palace court; they too observed a religious silence. The ambassador was introduced; he bowed. For a long time he had been polishing a little compliment, from which he promised himself the best results. But he had hardly opened his mouth when a volley of insults fell upon him. The idol was no longer hieratical: it was most definitely shouting and threatening.

'Otto is nothing but a traitor, a cunning scoundrel! He will pay dearly for taking two-thirds of Italy, for having designs on Greater Greece . . . etc., etc.!'

Liudprand tried to excuse his sovereign. But it is very doubtful whether he did in fact reply as he said he did: 'You have no rights over Greater Greece, Nicephorus, and you would be well advised to cede it to my glorious master!' For he would certainly have emerged from the interview at least with his eyes put out or his tongue cut. But whatever he said must have been unacceptable for Nicephorus suddenly cut short the interview with words which, incidentally, show how early a Basileus got up in the morning. 'It is already eight o'clock and I must go to Hagia Sophia for the day's solemn procession. You may go.'

Poor Nicephorus! He—and the interview—were to receive harsh treatment in the report which Liudprand wrote that evening for his beloved sovereign. Here is a realistic sketch, but scarcely an impartial one, of the Eastern Emperor. 'Imagine,' he wrote, 'a man of an appearance wholly that of an adventurer, reminiscent of a pigmy, with a big head, little pig eyes, and disfigured by a thick beard; short, fat and grizzled, with a hideously long neck. His long thick hair makes him resemble a pig. His face is the colour of an Ethiopian's, and altogether one would not like to meet him in the middle of the night. I must add that he has a swollen stomach, narrow hips, thighs much too long for his short stature, short legs, and disproportionate feet. He was dressed in a precious ceremonial garment, but it was very old, the colour was faded and it smelled as if it had been worn too much. In his speech he is insolent. He has the character of a fox. In his lies and perjury he is a Ulysses.'

As for the procession, this is how Liudprand chose to describe it: 'A great crowd of merchants and the people were assembled to acclaim Nicephorus; it filled both sides of the street which leads from the Palace to St Sophia, and looked like two walls made of ridiculously small shields and lamentable lances. The indecorum of this procession was the greater because, in order to honour the Emperor, most of the plebeians were bare-footed. But the court dignitaries who passed with him through the lines of bare-footed people were dressed in ill-fitting clothes, so old that many had holes in them. There was not a single man whose grandfather would have bought such a garment. No one was wearing gold or precious stones except perhaps Nicephorus who, dressed in State clothes which had been made for his predecessors, looked even more repulsive. I swear by your life, which is more precious to me than my own, that the ceremonial dress of one of your nobles is more valuable than a hundred of these.

'And as he advanced on a monster of a horse, the psalmists cried with base flattery, "Here is the Morning Star! The source of light rises! His look reflects the sun's rays! May the Autocrator Nicephorus live long! Render homage!" How much more appropriate if they had chanted "Here is the old man, the old fool, shuffling about like an old woman, as ugly as a satyr! Oh you lout, oh you clumsy one! Hairy old barbarian, broken-winded old oaf! The insolent, the shaggy one! You coarse old Cappadocian!" '

After the ceremony came the solemn banquet, to which Liudprand was invited. But he was given only fifteenth place, and that not even on the side of the table-cloth. His suite, moreover, was not allowed into the banqueting hall at all. The oily dishes made his stomach heave, the wine burned his inside and he was nauseated by the fish sauce. 'A veritable banquet of drunkards,' he exclaimed later, 'stinking of oil and fish.' In any case Nicephorus asked him so many questions that he hardly had time to eat. First the Basileus inquired about the forces that Otto had in Italy and the territories he had conquered. Then he suddenly burst out laughing: 'Your master's soldiers neither know how to fight on foot nor stay on their horses. They have no idea of the art of war. Their swords are so long, their shields so large, their helmets and armour so heavy, that they can hardly move and totter at every step. And as for your navy, it exists in name only! Mine, on the other hand, is invincible. It is on the sea that I shall conquer you!'

Otto's recent setbacks were naturally not forgotten and formed the subject of loud witticisms. 'You who could not even take the little town of Bari, how could you resist me with as many warriors behind me as there are grains of wheat on the plains of Gargare, grapes in Lesbos, waves on the sea and stars in the sky?' And then the supreme argument: 'Besides, you are not Romans. At the most you are Longobards!' Ingenuously Liudprand replied that he much preferred to be a Longobard, for no one could really deny that Rome was founded by a fratricidal bastard and a collection of insolvent debtors, fugitive slaves and people condemned to death. Why indeed should he blush on being called a Longobard when in the West the word Roman was associated only with the worst vices—treachery, laziness, greed, debauchery and falsehood?

Perhaps this reply was made in all innocence, but the effect on those present was electric. On a look from Nicephorus, Liudprund was seized and ejected. From this moment he was held under close supervision in the Marble Palace. The sun came through holes in roof and walls and by day the heat was overwhelming. At night there was much rain and frost and the ambassador was either soaked or chilled. He had nothing to drink but bitter wine. He had no pillows or covers and had to sleep on the hard stone. Courage was not his most obvious quality and already he saw himself about to die in this foreign land. He was reduced to tears and one morning sent an imploring message to Leo Phocas. 'Let us bring these negotiations to an end, or send me back to Italy.' Four days later the *curopalate* summoned him to the Sacred Palace. Trembling with fever he was brought before a group resembling an *areopagus*. Other solemn officials present in addition to Leo were Basil[1] the *parakimomenus*, Symeon the author of a famous novella, John Tzimisces, Sisinnos the urban prefect and the Master of the Robes. 'All very wise and learned men and as sweet as Attic honey,' wrote Liudprand ironically on returning home in the evening.

The interview started gently. 'Remind us, brother, why you have taken the trouble of coming thus far.' Forcing himself to keep calm, Liudprand again explained the purpose of his mission. On hearing what he said, everyone chuckled and exclaimed. 'You mean that you are asking for the hand of a *porphyrogenita* for the son of Otto?'[2] They turned to one another as though to make sure of such an extravagant idea. 'The *porphyrogenita* of a *porphyrogenitus*, that is the daughter born in the purple room to an Emperor who was himself born in the purple room—united with a barbarian king!'

Liudprand felt anger rise within him. No, indeed, he did not understand this determination to treat the proposed marriage as a misalliance. There was a precedent: Marie-Irene, the daughter of the Emperor Christopher, had been given in marriage to Peter, King of the Bulgars.

'Doubtless,' they replied in all seriousness, 'but this is not a comparable case. Theophano, for whose hand you are petitioning, is a *porphyrogenita*: she came to the world in the purple, of a father already crowned. Marie-Irene was not a *porphyrogenita*, for she was born *before* the elevation to the throne of her grandfather, Romanus Lecapenus.'

Weak with illness and exasperated, the unhappy bishop tried to protest. In a lengthy discourse which at first the Byzantines pretended to follow attentively, he made a historical survey. He

[1] The man who had helped Nicephorus to seize power.
[2] This was the name given to a princess of the blood, for she was 'born in the purple'.

spoke of the shameful yoke from which Rome had been delivered by the Germans; he recalled the gifts which his august master had bestowed upon the Vatican. His discourse ran away with him; he talked heedlessly, not noticing that no one was listening to him. And suddenly great shouts of laughter interrupted his confused oration. In a moment he was dismissed and was being hustled back to his palace.

On June 29 he was once more ordered out of it to attend the Feast of the Holy Apostles. The poor prelate was exhausted, but he had to stand for several hours, listening to endless songs and *cantilenae*. The ceremony, like all the others, was followed by a banquet. Here again the arrangements gave him grounds for complaint, for the places of honour at the diplomats' table were reserved for the envoys of the Bulgarian king, rough men who had not yet lost their wild ways. When he saw this, Liudprand angrily left the room. The master of ceremonies, the Emperor's brother and the Secretary of State ran after him. 'Why are you running away?' they shouted. 'Since Petrus, the King of the Bulgars, married the daughter of Emperor Christopher we have had an arrangement by which the ambassadors of the Bulgars must be accorded the highest rank at court and take precedence over the ambassadors of all other peoples. This Bulgarian is rough and badly washed and wears an iron belt, as you point out, but amongst us he has the rank of a patrician and it would not be fitting to place a bishop above him, particularly a Frank.'

This explanation naturally did not appease Liudprand, who refused to go back into the banqueting hall and asked leave to go home. But he was not allowed to go home; instead he was invited to share a meal with the servants in the Palace hostel. But, from his high seat Nicephorus had heard the scuffle and after learning the details he had a few choice dishes taken from his own table to the hostel for the bishop, to calm his righteous resentment. Liudprand, who was in fact something of a gourmand, made a rather touching reference to 'roast of fat young goat of which the Emperor himself had partaken, stuffed with garlic, onions and leeks and served with garos', the famous caviare sauce.

A few days later he received another invitation to dine at the Sacred Palace. The Bulgarians had gone and this time Liudprand sat in the place of honour. Other guests were the Patriarch Polyeuctes and numerous bishops. At a given moment the head of the Orthodox Church graciously asked 'the eminent Latin prelate' for some of his observations, in his official capacity, on Holy Scriptures. Liudprand assures us that he offered a dissertation 'elegant in form and very much to the point'. Then the Patriarch inquired about the number of councils recognized in the West. When Liudprand had enumerated them, Polyeuctes remarked that he had forgotten to mention the Saxon Council, and added with a burst of laughter, 'No wonder, since the canons it issued are still so new and there seems to be so little to be said for them that they have not yet reached us here!' Then the conversation turned to the other grievance which Byzantium had against the West—the Pope's refusal to recognize her supremacy in religious matters. Later on, in his report, Liudprand claimed to have made a crushing reply. 'All heresies have been born in the East and only in the West have they been condemned. As for our council which it pleases you to deride as the Saxon Council, at least it reminded us that it is more glorious to fight with the sword than with the pen and better to perish fighting than with back turned to the enemy. Your soldiers will find that out whenever you wish.'

But all these quarrels fatigued and unnerved the unhappy bishop and his stomach disorders got worse. He had more and more to complain about in the behaviour of the court. Sometimes they summoned him under the slightest pretext twice in one day. Then he would be left as though forgotten for several weeks at a time in his prison with his five Italian guards, brutes more suited to handling a lance or a sword than associating with an elegant and cultured prelate. His request to go home was never discussed. As the poor ambassador got thinner and thinner he piteously bemoaned his fate. 'I am so pale and unwell,' he wrote in his report, 'that when I go out, women turn to look pityingly at me.' Moreover he was running short of money, for—a detail symbolic of Byzantine avarice—he must pay not only for the needs of himself and his suite, but for those of his five gaolers. The Imperial officials certainly seemed to take pleasure in exhausting him. One day Nicephorus summoned him to the Figi Palace; and he who could hardly stand on his feet was made to listen, motionless for several hours, to a severe dressing down. Then he was dismissed, recalled and finally detained to dinner. On this occasion he met the father of Nicephorus, Bardas Phocas, now ninety years old and as wrinkled and decrepit as a two hundred years old mummy. 'Nevertheless,' he wrote that evening, 'the Greeks in their praises, or rather, their blustering, shout to him that they hope that God may prolong his days. From that alone, we can see how mad, greedy and foolish they are! On behalf of a man who is not merely old, but tottering on the brink of the grave, they ask what they know cannot be granted.'

In his marble prison the days went monotonously by. Recluse that he was, he did not know what was afoot; he did not know for example that while Nicephorus was apparently negotiating with him, he was dealing with Otto's rival Adalbert. So it was with astonishment that from the roof of his house, he saw an impressive fleet of twenty-four *chelandia*, two Russian and two Frankish vessels, under the command of a certain eunuch, set sail for Apulia and Calabria. Angrily he noted in his report, 'You may believe me that four hundred of our warriors would be enough to conquer this entire army, unless they dug themselves in behind walls or in trenches. In order to insult you, Nicephorus has appointed as commander a certain man—I say "certain" because he has ceased to be a man yet cannot become a woman.'

Finally came the blessed day when he was told—by Nicephorus himself—that he was to be allowed to leave. Byzantium was about to take up arms against the Arabs; on the very next day the Basileus left his capital and with great pomp went to take command of the Syrian army. Liudprand had certain observations to offer on this campaign. 'It is not so much a military campaign,' he wrote to his sovereigns, 'as an expedition to procure wheat. The Greek Empire, by the will of God, is at present suffering under such a famine that in this country where, in ordinary times, abundance is the rule, a golden piece will not buy a half measure of wheat. Nicephorus himself, allied with the rats in the fields, has aggravated the situation, for at harvest time he bought all the wheat in the Empire at a derisory price, accumulated grain thus like the sands of the seashore and stored it. After having prepared the most dreadful famine by this shameful commerce he assembled 80,000 men under the pretext that they were needed for a military campaign and for a whole month sold to them for two pieces of gold what he had bought for one. Such are the reasons, my lord, which have induced Nicephorus at the present time to lead his army against the Assyrians. But what an army! These are not men, but phantoms. . . . Nicephorus is not interested in their quality, but only in their number. One day he will see how dangerous this attitude is and too late he will repent; for these numerous cowards, who gain courage only from their numbers, will be exterminated by our warriors, less numerous, but skilled in war and, indeed, thirsting for it.'

Nicephorus, however, was reluctant to let him go without seeing him once more and summoned him to Brya, one of the stages on the route to Syria, on Sunday, July 26. Liudprand arrived full of confidence, for he had just been received at the Sacred Palace by the *curopalate* Leo. Leo had overwhelmed him with attention, embraced him and sworn, by the life of the Emperor, by his own life and the life of his children, that Liudprand's departure was imminent. The Greeks, Liudprand noted, were always very ready to swear by the lives of their closest relatives. But he was scarcely in the presence of the Basileus than he was given a thorough dressing down! Otto was a rascal and a knave and solely responsible for the indiscipline of the Longobardian princes Landolf of Beneventum and Pandolf of Capua. He was fit only for the gallows, etc., etc. Liudprand tried to reply but, as he wrote later in his diary, 'swollen like an angry toad, Nicephorus imposed silence upon me.' But once again it ended in an invitation to dine. Amongst the guests were two Italians: the brother of the princes of Beneventum and Capua, who was on bad terms with his family, and an envoy of the *strategos* of Longobardia. The entire meal was accompanied by insulting allusions to Otto, to the Latins and the Germans. Liudprand had to endure it all in silence. Towards the end of the meal Nicephorus spoke of the hunt organized for the next day. 'Admit your master does not possess a park as pleasant as mine!' he said, turning to the Bishop of Cremona. The bishop protested. 'And has he any wild asses?' This time Liudprand had to admit that he had not. Pleased with having scored a point Nicephorus invited Liudprand to join the hunt on the following morning.

So our dyspeptic prelate was obliged to play the part of Nimrod. Over hill and dale they made him go. The terrain was rough and broken up by deep forests, and the unfortunate ambassador, sick and feverish, could only groan. Then suddenly someone noticed that the bishop was wearing a hood. An unheard of scandal! A hood in the Emperor's presence! He had to take it off and wear a *teristra*. This was too much for his poor nerves, and he blurted out, 'It is all very well for women to wear these things, but when we Westerners go on horseback we wear a hood. Please allow us to follow our own customs as we would allow you to follow yours if you came to stay with us. We tolerate all your eccentricities of costume and usage—your ridiculously long hair, your clothes like women's, your robes with long sleeves and big checks. We even allow you to salute our princes with your heads covered, a thing unheard of. Leave us then to our own ways!' And Liudprand refused to do as requested. Consequently he was told to leave the hunt, to get out of the park. He did not have to be told twice.

On July 27, the next day, the Basileus confirmed that he had permission to leave, and he returned joyfully to Constantinople. But in the capital he was told by a serious-faced young official that because the activities of Saracen pirates made the seas unsafe at that time, the administration, in the interests of his own safety, must withhold from him permission to leave for the time being. A thunderbolt falling at his feet would perhaps not have shaken Liudprand more. This setback, which was probably a practical joke, was to have very serious consequences; for a few days later a very important event took place.

On the day of the Assumption two envoys of Pope John XIII unexpectedly arrived in Constantinople. They too were commissioned to arrange the marriage and—oh, horror—in their credentials Otto was described as Emperor of the Romans and Nicephorus as Emperor of the Greeks. Such sacrilege, everyone felt, should have caused the ship to be swallowed up by the waves! The reaction was immediate: the plenipotentiaries were thrown into prison, whipped and tortured. While all this was going on Liudprand was summoned to the Palace; trembling, he was received by the eunuch Christophoros. But the latter held out a friendly hand. Perhaps he was softened by the bishop's dejected manner, the pallor of his face, his drawn features, his too-long hair and his unshaven chin. Christophoros began by apologizing very politely for the delay attending the Bishop's voyage. The blame must be placed firmly upon the Pope's envoys, whose impudence had turned the court completely upside down.

Then the conversation changed. 'In fact, how insolent they are! This Pope is indeed bold! It is true that he is pushed on by Otto. Luxury, pretence, infamy—that is what the German monarchy and the Vatican amount to!'

Gradually, as Christophoros became intoxicated by the sound of his own voice, the conversation became more heated. Liudprand was no longer in doubt: he too would be thrown into a dark prison, there to perish, eaten by rats. 'It was not premeditated', he murmured awkwardly.

But the eunuch did not want to be convinced, and repeated, 'Nicephorus alone has the right to call himself Roman Emperor. After the departure of Constantine the Great, Rome was inhabited only by slaves and bastards. All honourable people fled to Byzantium.'

Liudprand did not really know what to do or say. 'You may believe me that it is all a misunderstanding. The Pope acted in good faith. You have renounced the clothes, the language and the manners of the Romans and he thought you misnamed. I promise you that another time the Pope will better understand how to draw up his letters.'

Then Christophoros stopped himself in the middle of a violent tirade and burst out laughing. 'Does your master still want this marriage?'

'Certainly he did want it,' replied Liudprand, 'but now that you unjustly hold me prisoner his fury will be extreme and he will not wish to hear it spoken of under any circumstances.'

'Then,' stormed the eunuch, 'we shall destroy his power! Even his distant and rustic homeland will not give him refuge against us. With our subsidies we shall assemble all the nations of the earth.'

The eunuch and the bishop politely took leave of one another, each assuring the other that his empire would be smashed 'like a pot'.

Liudprand was led back to his prison, the Marble Palace; now he was subjected to a régime of total seclusion. Beggars of Latin origin came to ask alms of him; they were beaten with rods and cast into prison. When an unknown friend or a charitable person sent him food—fruit or spices or good Italian wine—his guards rushed in, threw the provisions into the dust and drove out the startled porters with blows of their fists. He expected to receive an order of execution at any moment.

But the representative of so powerful a monarch could not be executed so easily, even if that monarch's title of 'Roman Emperor' could not be admitted. In fact, the longed-for day of release was not now far off.

But one more insult was in store for him. Digging into his baggage, the Imperial customs officers suddenly noticed five pieces of purple cloth of very great value. 'I have special permission to buy them and to take them back to Italy', the bishop hastened to point out.

'Do you not know that these are "prohibited" goods, much too beautiful for barbarians, and reserved for subjects of the Empire?' Having said this the officers confiscated the cloth.

Liudprand was very distressed. He pointed out that on the occasion of his first mission twenty years previously, when he was only a deacon and did not represent the great Otto, he had been allowed to take out similar fine silken goods. In vain he turned to the *curopalate* Leo and Evodision the interpreter, both of whom had been present when Nicephorus had formally given him permission to buy sacerdotal cloths and materials.

Then he exploded. 'You can put up all the obstacles you like, but it won't stop Oriental goods reaching the West! Whatever you do, the merchants of Amalfi and Venice will always know how to get for our clergy and prostitutes these things which in your mad and ignorant vanity you think are reserved for you alone! They will go on making fortunes out of this commerce which you imagine you monopolize.'

The only result of this outburst was that instead of confiscating only the five disputed items, the customs officers took possession of everything he had bought or received, prohibited or not.

In return they solemnly handed him two letters. One was for Otto: a chrysograph, or missive written in golden letters, signed in red ink by the Emperor and sealed with the great golden bull. The other was for Pope John XIII: an argyrograph, written in silver letters and sealed by the silver bull, but, and this was a deliberate insult, it was signed by Leo, the Emperor's brother. To the German Emperor the Byzantine court repeated the statement made so often to his ambassador: the condition of the marriage was the evacuation of Italy and the punishment of the rebel princes of Capua and Beneventum. In the argyrograph the Pope was ordered to cease describing himself as the universal pontiff and to remember that he was simply the Bishop of Rome.

When the moment of leave-taking came, everyone put up a great show of affection. They embraced Liudprand, they hoped that his stay had not been too disagreeable, they hoped that they would have the honour of seeing him again very soon, etc., etc. All the same, when he asked for horses for himself and his suite a thousand difficulties were raised; eventually a few saddle horses were brought along but his request for pack-horses was categorically refused. The palace drogman who conveyed them did not hesitate to demand the highest price. In short, the vexations continued to the very end. Liudprand in return had to be content with writing insulting remarks on the walls of his prison and the composition of a satirical poem in mediocre hexameters.

He was pursued by misfortune on his journey home, which was full of tragi-comic incidents.

For fear of pirates he dared not embark from Byzantium, but travelled overland to the Greek port of Naupactos (Lepanto). And so for 49 days, assailed by hunger and thirst, he travelled on donkey or on horseback across an arid land. But he was sustained by the joy of having left 'that accursed city, formerly rich and flourishing above all, today half-starved and inhabited by a people perjured, lying, deceitful, rapacious and grasping to a degree'.

Arriving in Naupactos, he found two Italian merchant ships on the point of sailing for Otranto. He at once blessed his good fortune. But he was to regret it.

Once at sea the captain sought him out and took possession of all his provisions for the journey. 'You see,' he explained, 'without the proper papers we cannot risk touching land to revictual.' Next a terrible storm arose in the Gulf of Patras; for two days they were battened down in the hold, without food and almost without water. Liudprand had abandoned all hope of survival when quite suddenly it all came clear to him. He had neglected to pray at the tomb of St Andrew, the patron of Patras! Immediately he threw himself to his knees and asked pardon. At once the waves died down and soon the ship reached the island of Leucadia. They had scarcely landed when the crews took the opportunity to disappear, and so the bishop was immobilized. He sought out the bishop's palace and went to visit his colleague. He found—oh horror!—a eunuch, and for a week he was the object of constant and malevolent inhospitality. But as a writer Liudprand was never without resources and he got his revenge by writing a harsh description of the local Byzantine clergy. 'All eager for money, all simonists, selling position and privilege.' However, his hatred for Nicephorus provided some excuse for them. 'It is true that every one of them is overwhelmed with taxation. Even the tiny diocese of Leucadia must pay a hundred bags of gold!'

Eventually, on December 14 the ships set sail for Corfu; the shortage of crew put the longer journey to Otranto out of the question. After three days the island appeared, but at that very moment a fearful earthquake occurred. When it was all over the travellers asked for, and were given permission to land. A few days later Liudprand was invited to dine with the *strategos*, Michael. The host was kindly and jovial. The guest remarked that when he was back in Northern Italy he would not forget the warmth of his welcome. Michael smiled: 'Why then leave so quickly? If you are happy here, stay!' To the great unhappiness of the bishop, these words in the course of a few days proved prophetic. When Liudprand expressed his intention of continuing his journey the governor, motivated by greed, used all sorts of pretexts to detain him. Days, then weeks, passed in this way. In the end the chamberlain Leo, who had been ordered by the court to conduct the bishop as far as Ancona in an Imperial ship, became angry and reclaimed his passenger. On January 7, 969,

Liudprand was able to resume his journey. The unhappy man soon discovered that he had exchanged one exploiter for another. The courier who conducted him aboard ship took a precious vase from him by force, and then tried to rob him. During the journey he discovered 'a horrible plot': the captain

FIG. 60

Gryphon seizing a lion: tapestry of the eleventh century preserved at Lyons Originally from the Church of St Gereon, Cologne

had been scheming to get rid of him by abandoning him on a desert island.

Finally, on January 10, 969, the worthy prelate reached

Ancona. He had completed an extraordinary mission lasting more than six months. It had been both painful and futile.

*　　*　　*

One day Byzantium was bitterly to regret the haughtiness with which, at the height of her power, she had treated the Latin West; for the year 1204, which brought the capture of Constantinople by the Crusaders, was not far off. But, above all, the day was to come which saw the arrival of Mahomet, the Turks, and the final collapse.

VI

THE GREAT CATASTROPHE

The Collapse of a Thousand Year Empire

Now the great tragedy began. Soon the Byzantine Empire would have ceased to exist. Mass would no longer be said in St Sophia. The memories of eleven centuries, the vestiges of an amazing grandeur, and the riches of an unimaginable beauty were to disappear from one day to the next as if swallowed up. In twenty-four hours the brilliance of Byzantium was replaced by the Turkish night.

It is always poignant to see the fall of an ancient empire, but this was an entire civilization that fell with the city walls, and a religion, our own. And in what circumstances! For a long time fate hesitated to pronounce a verdict. For a long time the outcome of the war was uncertain. And but for an almost incredible series of misfortunes the Crescent would never have supplanted the Cross. The ultimate tragedy—and this makes it even more poignant—was by no means inevitable.

At dawn on April 5, 1453, a deafening noise was heard. 'The God-protected town' woke up suddenly and all fit

FIG. 61

Capital from Hagia Sophia

men hastened to the battlements. A frightful sight met their eyes. Along the entire length of the great rampart known as the land wall, from the Sea of Marmora to the Golden Horn, wherever one looked, to the horizon or far along the coasts, an army as numerous as the sands of the sea had pitched its tents.

The Turks! Squadrons and battalions were calling to one another and making an immense clamour, and with a dull rumble cannon were slowly moved into position. Thousands of animals were bellowing. There was a clatter of arms, and above it all, from time to time, the strident notes of the kettle-drum and side-drum. This was one of the momentous scenes of history: thousands of fateful warriors pressing round the walls of Byzantium in the spring of 1453. There were, in fact, 200,000 men, but the number was soon to increase to half a million. There were the numerous soldiers of the regular army—for all Turks must do military service; there were the Bashi-bazouks—those irregulars of every race and religion, too poor to possess horses, and apparently all the more reckless as a result. There were above all the Janissaries, an *élite* corps with the harshest discipline, which had given the Turkish army an assured supremacy since the beginning of the century. It is one of the ironies of history that their ranks were made up only of captured Christian children, taken from conquered nations!

A host of standards clapped in the wind. One of gold and red silk, planted on an eminence, stood out; this was the standard of Mahomet II, a young man of twenty-three, cold, stubborn and ambitious, who had sworn to take the city. It was certain that no scruple would stop him. On the day after he came to power he had his younger brother drowned in order to eliminate a possible rival; it was on the day too—a thoughtful gesture—on which his mother arrived from her distant province to greet him. There had been a state of latent war between the two empires ever since his accession. With a complete disregard for treaties he had already built the formidable castle fortress of Roumeli Hissar on the Greek shore of the Bosphorus at the narrowest point of the straits, with the object of preventing Byzantium from getting provisions by sea. On November 26, 1452, a Venetian ship laden with barley had to its cost tried to force a way through. The great bronze cannon soon immobilized it. Barbaro, a Venetian chronicler of the siege, has told us what happened to the crew. 'The owner of the ship, Antonio Rizzo, was taken from the water and sent to the Turkish lord of Adrianople and imprisoned. After fourteen days the lord had him impaled on a stake. As for a son of Domenigo de Maestris, the ship's writer, he put him, alas, into his *seraglio*. Some of the sailors were allowed to go on to Constantinople. The others were cut in two.'

On this day, then, Mahomet had simply cast aside all pretence and everyone behind the ramparts knew that the hour of decision had arrived. Besides, the Sultan hastened to dispel any remaining doubts. As soon as the midday prayer was over, during which, with mats unrolled and faces turned towards Mecca, the whole of this immense army gave itself up to rhythmic movements of worship, he dispatched *tellals*, or heralds, into the camp to proclaim among the tents the famous news. 'The siege of the city has begun.' The siege of 1453: the siege which was not to be lifted—one of the most dramatic in history. . . .

Simultaneously, the Turkish fleet, until then concentrated on Gallipoli, came quickly through the Sea of Marmora and arrived in the Bosphorus: 493 ships, armed to the teeth, the largest armada, affirmed Critobulus, that had ever yet been seen.

Four hundred thousand men on one side, then, and nearly 500 ships, and on the other side . . . 8,000 men and 15 ships! For the Eastern Empire was indeed only a shadow of its former self. It had never recovered from the terrible blow which it sustained at the hands of the Crusaders at the beginning of the thirteenth century and its territorial power was limited, so to speak, to the few miles represented by the circumference of Byzantium. In order to reach these walls from their capital, Adrianople, it had only been necessary for the Turks to cross a few miles of undefended country. Byzantium, indeed, had some troops, but they were far away in the Balkans and the Peloponnese, immobilized by the enemy. She could not count on them. Worse still, the 8,000 men inside the town included many monks and volunteers who had no military training whatsoever. Only 5,000 were Greeks; the others had spontaneously hastened to the threatened city to support Christianity against Islam.

Again, of the 15 ships 10 were Italian—they had by a miracle got through the barrage of Roumeli Hissar. Some were pirates who had volunteered their services; others were mere provision ships, forcefully retained to take part in the defence of the town. Thus, the inequality of means was enormous; nevertheless only an extraordinary succession of events, often unforeseen, was to bring victory to the Turks. For despite everything the Byzantines had many trump cards to play.

Their generalissimo, John Giustiniani, was an outstanding man. This Genoese nobleman had rushed to the threatened town. Energetic, bold, intelligent, he had a great reputation in the Christian world. More than once during the siege he was to withhold victory from the Turks.

If many of his troops were of poor quality, he had 700 of his own Genoese: 300 sailors and 400 soldiers 'dressed in iron'— in coats of mail, that is. He had some captains of wide experience, for the most part Italians: Contarini, Corner, Mocenigo, Dolfin, Trevisan, the Bocchiardi brothers and Aloisio Diedo. His fleet was composed mostly of ships of the line of high hull for which the little Turkish *fustes* were no match unless they were present in large numbers. And it was due to Giustiniani that Byzantium had two corsairs available, one of 2,300 tons and the other of 800.

Then she had the chain-boom. The whole Eastern world knew about this famous contrivance, several hundreds of feet long and made of great rounded logs fastened together with iron hooks. When stretched across the Channel of the Golden Horn and firmly secured on both banks from the wall of Constantinople to the Galata shore,[1] no armada could make its way through. Behind the boom there was safe anchorage for the fleet; and as for the garrison, it need not watch the section of the wall facing the Channel.

In addition Byzantium was encircled by high fortifications. More grandiose than those of Rome, stouter than those of Avignon, much more extensive and impressive than those of Carcassonne or Aigues-Mortes, they alone through the centuries had reduced to nothing a thousand barbarian attempts to destroy the city. They consisted of two parallel walls, the inner one strengthened by 112 great square towers. Moreover for half their length, for two sides of the triangle they formed, they fell straight into the sea: the Sea of Marmora to the west and the Channel of the Golden Horn to the east, the latter sealed by the boom. It is true that most of the construction was ancient,

---

[1] Neutral territory. The Genoese had secured a concession over Galata and its hinterland for the purposes of commerce.

dating back to the reign of Theodosius II in the fifth century, and many points were in need of restoration. A recent attempt to rebuild had been sabotaged by negligent engineers. Only the outside wall had been repaired to some extent by John Palaeologus between 1433 and 1444. However, during recent weeks the garrison had worked hard to make good the most obvious weaknesses, stopping up gaps here, digging there. So it was that in March, led by the Basileus, everyone set to work to clear out the great foss in the region of the Hebdomon Palace, 'the one point', Barbaro explains, 'where the land wall was indeed very weak'. The Venetian chronicler has left us a colourful account of this work.

'The Basileus asked Aloiso Diedo, the captain of the three galleys which had come from Tana, kindly to go with his galleys and crews to the end of the Golden Horn, there to fortify the said Palace and to dig in front of this end portion of the wall a moat a hundred feet wide and eight feet deep. Diedo replied that he would happily undertake this work. "Firstly," he said to the Emperor, "for the honour of God and all Christianity; and also for love of your Empire, which is in danger of being conquered by the Turk. So must your land be strong. On Monday morning I will raise anchor and will sail towards the port of Kynegion. There we shall disembark and stoutly each one will dig his part of the ditch." And when Monday arrived which was the fourteenth day of the month of March, it was even as the captain had promised and when the ships had arrived at the designated place, everyone disembarked with a good will, bearing pickaxes, spades and baskets for moving earth. The Emperor and all his baronage were standing there to contemplate this good work and the master of each galley had fixed his banner in the earth as a point of assembly for his men and on this day the greater part of the moat was dug so willingly did every man work, first for the love of God, then for fear of the Turk so that he could not quickly approach the walls. When the evening came the Emperor warmly thanked the captain for the good work which he had done in the name of the Seignory of Venice. My lord Gabriel Trevisan and the crews of his two light galleys also worked until the setting of the sun, digging the moat and fortifying the Palace walls.'

Until March 31 everyone worked uninterruptedly, constantly fearing a sudden enemy attack. But guards posted on the neighbouring hill did not have to give the alarm. 'By the grace of God,' said Barbaro, 'no one came. In the evening, at about the hour of compline, the moat was completed and the Italian galleys of Aloisio Diedo and their valiant crews returned to their anchorage off Pera.'

Moreover, still faithful to her diplomatic habits, Byzantium had employed corruption. The second personage of the Ottoman Empire, the Grand Vizir Khalil Pasha, was in her pay. Through him she was kept informed of the enemy's intentions and through his influence she hoped that the siege might be lifted.

FIG. 62

Sculptured slab

Finally, the supreme hope: Byzantium counted on the West. If only the Pope, or Venice, or Genoa would only send a fleet, the Infidels would have to withdraw. Were these hopes so vain? Neither of these great republics, mistresses of Levantine commerce, would care to see the Straits fall under the sway of the Sultan; and the Sovereign Pontiff could not rejoice in a victory of the Crescent over the Cross. Doubtless in the past relations between His Holiness and the 'Equal of the Apostles' had not been very cordial; for a long time the latter had affected to regard the former as a simple bishop, the former had never for one moment deigned to consider the remonstrances of the distant sovereign. Even more serious, Roman Catholicism and the Orthodox Church no longer recognized the same canons, and charged one another with deviationism. But faced with the Turkish peril the Basileus had made many concessions. At the Council of Florence in 1439 he had agreed in the name of his people to abjure certain of his beliefs and to bring about a union of the two churches. So it was that during the last days of 1452 a solemn ceremony had taken place in St Sophia to mark the end of the great schism. Basileus, Pontifical Legate and Patriarch of Constantinople, had officiated in great pomp, assisted by 300 priests. There had been a solemn procession of reliquaries in the presence of the body of St Spiridion, whose day it was. It would be an exaggeration to say that this reconciliation was popular; indeed, crowds in the streets had protested against the blasphemy of it. In the depths of his dark cell in the Monastery of the Pantocrator, between his prayers and macerations, the celebrated monk George Scholarios maintained a long denunciation of the abjuration. A party, the Zealots, was formed whose members advocated 'death to the azymites and their idolatry'. But it was this very sacrifice, this renunciation of an essential point of doctrine, that Byzantium hoped would be rewarded.

Now that the weaknesses and the strengths of the two sides have been described, we must watch the progress of this famous siege. It was punctuated by dramatic events; it was anything but monotonous. When Byzantium finally succumbed, the Turk owed his victory more than anything else—on such details does destiny depend—to the unreliability of the winds. . . .

The Capture and Sack of Constantinople by the Turks

It was then, on April 5 that the Turks appeared under the walls of Constantinople. On the 6th and 7th they moved closer to the land ramparts, first within a mile and then three-quarters. On the 9th, as a security measure, the Byzantines moved their nine largest vessels up to the boom, with their poops to the battle.

On the 10th and 11th nothing happened, but two events of unequal importance occurred on the 12th. The Turkish fleet, having arrived in the Bosphorus, went to anchor at a place called the Two Columns, just below the Dolma Bagcha Palace of today. The garrison greatly feared a sudden attack; naval preparations were speeded up and sentries were posted on the Pera wall. 'And this is why,' wrote Barbaro, 'we were in such a great fright, that night and day we stood at arms, although this fleet never moved. But even so it kept us on the alert from April 12 to May 29, eight weeks day and night.'

But a much more serious event occurred on April 12, which brought consternation to the defender. The great Turkish gun, the Basilic, went into action for the first time. This monster well merited its nickname, 'the Royal One', if only on account of the number of its attendants. One hundred pairs of oxen dragged it, 100 men were in attendance on each side to support it, 200 workers flattened the road for it and 50 carpenters were ready for any event. In certain sources there are even references to 2,000 workers. It had taken two months and an escort of 10,000 soldiers to complete the relatively short journey from Adrianople to Constantinople. Its barrel was three feet in diameter and it fired projectiles weighing 1,500 lb. On the occasion of its first trial at Adrianople the Sultan took good care to warn the population so as 'to avoid frightening pregnant women'. The noise was heard 13 miles away and the projectile made a crater six feet deep. This great gun had been made by a turncoat Hungarian Christian called Orban, or Urban, formerly in the service of Byzantium. This, perhaps, is the first example of the bad luck which pursued the Greeks all through the siege. For if the walls of the city had been more robust the Byzantines would have been able to use more cannon—each shot fired caused a crack— and so give Urban more work to do and pay him more. For the cause of his desertion was simply under-employment and too little pay. And what dreadful consequences followed! With an infernal noise, followed by a trail of smoke and dust, great projectiles hurtled over day after day, smashing the ramparts and demolishing them. These fortifications, a source of such confidence and pride, for more than a thousand years had served Byzantium as an impregnable shield. Now, on the morning of April 12, it was obvious to everyone that under such blows they were doomed. Words cannot describe the garrison's anguish. And what additional fatigue this meant to the defenders! At all hours, even in the night, men and women, children and old persons had to turn out to fill new breaches in the wall. There was no respite for an instant, for the gun was never silent for long. We may imagine the state of physical ruin to which the already nerve-wracked defenders were reduced by such constant watch and effort. And yet they would need all the strength they could muster on the day, the fateful day, that the decisive assault was launched.

After a week of bombardment the fortifications were down at certain points. In the Lycus valley, the most vulnerable place in the defences, a part of the outer wall, and then two great towers on the inner wall, were broken down. Even worse, the debris had partly filled the moat. The Sultan was now quite certain that the city was at his mercy. On the 18th, two hours after sunset, he launched his assault troops. This first attack has been related by Barbaro:

'On the eighteenth day of this same month of April a great multitude of Turks came to the walls. This took place at about two o'clock in the night and the fight lasted until six o'clock in the night, that is, until six hours after sunset, and in this combat many Turks perished. And when these Turks approached the walls it was dark, and this enabled them to approach unexpectedly without being noticed. But do not ask me with what and how many cries they flung themselves at the walls or how they were able to retain their drums so that there seemed to be many more Turks than there actually were. Their cries were heard even on the coast of Asia Minor, twelve miles from their camp. And while they were making these terrible cries the Emperor began to weep in his sorrow and anxiety that this night the Turk might make a general assault, that we were not yet sufficiently prepared. That is why the Emperor knew this great anxiety. But Eternal God would not on this occasion permit such a great abomination and at six o'clock the fight ended and quiet reigned again to the great shame and very great losses of those pagans!

The repulse of this attack was almost entirely the work of Giustiniani and his 700 'armoured' men. They alone had sustained the shock of these frenzied assaults. A great victory then for the garrison! On the next day the Basileus, the Patriarch and all his clergy went to Saint Sophia to sing a thanksgiving.

Hardly was this alert over, hardly had each side finished collecting its dead, the Christians to bury them, the Moslems to burn them, than the Sultan, always on the alert, had worked out a new move. And so, on the next day, amidst angry shouts, 300 of his armed ships, in full sail, flung themselves on the famous chain-boom in an attempt to force it. Let Critobulus describe the event in his own picturesque words:

'Reducing their speed when they were within range of missiles and arrows, the enemy in their turn had recourse to weapons which can be thrown from afar. One struck and one was struck. These weapons were arrows and stone bullets from guns. Then the Turkish fleet rushed as near as possible to the Greek vessels which were ranged in line behind the Chain. From the decks of their ships a party of Turkish soldiers dressed in armour and with torches in their hands tried to set fire to the Greek ships in the port. Others incessantly shot fire arrows at them. Others tried to cut the anchor ropes. Yet others with hooks and ladders climbed up the sides of the ships. Others, by means of axes, javelins and long lances, killed the Christian sailors. And all showed high spirits and extreme courage in action. The object of all this effort was to repel, to set fire to or to sink the Christian vessels in order to break the famous Chain.

'The Christian crews were prepared in advance for this attack and due to the far-sightedness of the Grand Duke Notaras, who commanded them, and of the commander of that section of the ramparts, they were supplied with the necessary equipment and they had the advantage of the superior height of their great ships. From this eminent position they covered the assailants with a continuous hail of stones, javelins, lances, darts and projectiles of all kinds. Especially those who had taken up a position

PLATE 14.
Fragments of the Imperial Palace preserved in the gardens of the old Seraglio at Istanbul

The only one of the imperial palaces still standing, that of Constantine Porphyrogenetus, now called Tekfur Serai, Istanbul

PLATE 15. *The walls of Byzantium:* (top) *Scene of the breach in 1453;* (centre) *the Marble Towers;* (bottom) *general view of the walls of Theodosius toward the Belgrade Gate*

on the poop or on the masts wreaked great carnage amongst their adversaries, killing and wounding a great number. They even had vessels full of water, dependent upon long ropes, with which they extinguished fires, and enormous stones which they let fall from on high to the enemy ships, which were drawn up almost to the very sides of theirs causing thus frightful injuries amongst the aggressors.

'The ardour of the combatants was extreme and the issue was always in doubt. The Turks wanted to force a way into the Golden Horn. The Christians, Greek and Italian, resisted bravely. After a fight as short as it was violent the Christian vessels, thanks to their heroic constancy, forced the Sultan's fleet to retire. The Turkish ships, abandoning on this occasion all hope of breaking the Chain, regained their anchorage at the Two Columns, followed by the insulting remarks, the jeers and the shouts of triumph of the Christian crews.'

A second victory for the Byzantines! But that evening the Sultan summoned the gunmakers and ordered them to construct a gun capable of sinking the Christian ships ranged at the entrance to the port. The craftsmen exclaimed, 'But how could we in so doing avoid hitting the walls of Galata?' Whereupon Mahomet, who seems to have been knowledgeable concerning ballistics, drew for them the plan of a piece of artillery for plunging fire. The engineers were won over and set to work at once. So it was that a few days later the Genoese in Galata were not a little alarmed to hear missiles whistling over their town. The first dropped into the sea, but the second fell on a ship which broke in two. Must the Greek ships abandon the defence of the port for fear of being sunk? Fortunately for the city this was not necessary for the ships were able to move slowly to a point out of range of the Sultan's gun, and were never hit again. The Turks were foiled once more.

* * *

And so dawned the dramatic day of April 20. During the afternoon sentries on the wall suddenly noticed four points on the horizon which soon revealed themselves as four large ships in full sail moving rapidly nearer. Their size alone indicated their origin; they were Christian ships and they were bringing men and supplies. The bells were pealed, calling the entire population to the ramparts. Reinforcements were coming at last! But joy faded, as the presence of the Turkish fleet was remembered. These four vessels were lost if the Turks saw them; the Byzantines looked from the horizon to the left, from the source of hope to the source of despair. But the ships quickly grew bigger and still all remained quiet. They approached the city and entered the narrows. In a few moments the four would be safe, for the enemy would not have time to get under way and bar their entrance to the Golden Horn. Hearts were beating faster; many people got down on their knees to invoke the help of God and the Blessed Virgin. Still the Turks had not moved. Then a thousand cries of dismay, a thousand fingers pointed to the Two Columns where, after all, there was a great deal of sudden activity. The Turkish fleet was preparing for action; the Christian vessels had been seen. And a moment later, like black vultures, the Sultan's ships passed rapidly under the eyes of the horrified garrison. There were more than 300 of them. On the decks could be seen thousands of archers, soldiers in helmets and armour and even Janissaries. Each vessel had a large assortment of firing and thrusting weapons; some even had culverins and the largest were surrounded by a wall of enormous shields as protection against javelins.

Still unaware of the extent of their danger the four vessels continued on their way. They had not yet seen the enemy that lay in wait. Slowly they approached the point of the Acropolis. They were sailing in a way that kept them as far as possible from the shore until the last moment. They were a fine sight with sails full of wind, high hulls and poops. They arrived before the city, turned and at that precise moment found themselves confronting the Turkish fleet. Amongst the Moslems there broke out a deafening row—men shouted, war drums rolled, trumpets emitted strident notes, all vying with one another to sound the death of their prey. 'Succeed or die', the Sultan had said to his admiral, Baltoglou, who was therefore among the most excited. But he first advanced cautiously to within firing range, and holding himself there, engaged in distant combat. Javelins and

THE GREAT CATASTROPHE

stones flew in both directions, burning arrows were shot at sails in the hope of starting fires. In an instant the sea was covered with debris of all kinds. Meanwhile the Christians put up a vigorous resistance; well protected by their coats of mail, perched high on their big ships, they poured an enormous weight of stone, shot and javelins on to the little Turkish *fustes*. Baltoglou was surprised by this resistance; he decided to cut short the preliminaries and sent his front line ships forward for boarding operations. Like a pack of unleashed hounds they rushed on with eager howls. But they were too low to hook on and the Latin vessels were borne on irresistibly by the wind, leaving wreckage and the bodies of Turkish sailors in their wake. Would the miracle happen? Would they escape the teeth of that immense fleet? They were only a few dozen yards from the Golden Horn and safety. From the ramparts thousands of pairs of eyes watched this unequal—yet uncertain—fight. And suddenly the wind dropped. The sails flapped loosely from the masts and the four ships, as Barbaro says, 'fell into a lull'. With shouts of joy like those of hounds getting their fangs into the prey, the Turkish *fustes* rushed upon them. Baltoglou was first and fastened on to the prow of the biggest ship. Soon the struggle was an infernal hand-to-hand. Critobulus has left us a vivid account of what happened!

'All rushed forward furiously in this terrible fight. Amongst the Turks, some with lighted torches in hand, ran to set fire to enemy ships, others tried with axes and javelins to break open the sides, still others by means of long lances tried from below to reach the Latin fighters, others, finally, sought to kill them with arrows or stones, or, gripping anchor chains or ropes, tried to climb up on deck. All fought with an indescribable fury, but to little effect. As for the Christian warriors, covered from head to foot with armour, placed high, in a favourable position, they repulsed all attacks with an unheard-of ardour. They had big vessels laden with water and with piles of stones on deck. The stones were thrown down upon their assailants. The water put out fires started by the enemy. Rocks crushed the Turkish soldiers or flung them into the sea where they drowned. With lance, dart, javelin and pike the Latins pierced those who tried to climb up or they cut off their hands with cutlasses. Others amongst them, armed with maces or iron bars, smote the assailants on the head, breaking their skulls. The naked bodies of some Turks were burned by Greek fire. The tumult of the battle was extraordinary. Cries of pain and of anger and the blasphemies of those in agony made an infernal noise. Men killed and were killed, men thrust forward ceaselessly; men blasphemed and insulted, threatened and cried with pain. . . .'

In the absence of wind the swell gradually carried the vessels towards Galata and Constantinople, so that eventually the combatants were only a stone's throw from the bank. There, in the Golden Horn, behind the boom, the crews of the Byzantine vessels were jumping with impatience, and despaired to see their comrades so near and yet to be unable to help them. As for the Sultan, he was on horseback, surrounded by his turbaned general staff, shouting encouragement from the bank. How could the unfortunate vessels escape? One had five galleys on its sides, another struggled with thirty *fustes*, yet another with forty. When a Turkish ship was knocked out it was immediately replaced by another. The whole sea was covered with craft and even the sky was obscured from time to time by a cloud of projectiles. The fierce battle had already lasted several hours. The centre of it all was undoubtedly the struggle between the Turkish admiral's galley and the great Imperial transport on which it had got its hooks. The other Christian ships, although assailed by a mass of Turkish boats, ceaselessly manoeuvred to protect it. They had succeeded in coming so close together that from afar, according to Phrantzes, they gave the illusion of being 'the four towers of one building'. But however they moved, they drew with them, as though hanging on to their flesh, a pack of boats which refused to let go. On one occasion Mahomet was so carried away with excitement that he leapt into the sea on horseback, followed by his Pashas and swam towards the ships which the current had then brought in near to the bank. He shouted and screamed, threatened and swore. This resistance exasperated him. He flung absurd orders at Baltoglou, who could only pretend not to hear. He addressed his admiral and his men as cowards. This must surely have been a strange spectacle:

cavalry with long *kaftans* floating behind them, mounted on swimming horses, manoeuvring furiously about amongst skiffs and galleys in the midst of a naval battle!

Then, smarting under their master's insults, Baltoglou and his sailors made a supreme effort. The sun was setting on the horizon and it was the sixth hour of the battle, but they flung themselves into the struggle with a new ardour. The Christians had repulsed many attacks and were growing weak; they could do little more, and the end seemed near. On the shore and on the ramparts this change was noticed. The Sultan welcomed it with a great shout of triumph, while on the ramparts desperate prayers were said. Christ and the Holy Virgin, could they then have abandoned their own? Then the miracle happened. The wind rose again, the sails filled proudly and the ships creaked with happiness. Now the great Genoan craft leaped ahead, their progress irresistible. Anything in their way was split or pounded or sunk and behind them was only the debris of ships, galleys, oars and tackle. The Turkish *fustes* fought back ferociously, but every moment they lost ground. Soon the Italians were out of reach. The wind had brought an end to the battle. While the Turks returned dismally to their anchorage, the Christian vessels, so marvellously saved, received in the harbour of the Golden Horn the kind of joyous welcome which is more easily imagined than described.

On the evening of April 20 the garrison gave itself up to rejoicing. But the Byzantines were celebrating a victory which it had been better not to have gained. Better by far would it have been for Byzantium if those four Italian ships had never reached port!

Pale with rage, Mahomet was back in his tent. The failure kept him awake all night. He pored over his maps: there was Byzantium and there was the Golden Horn where, well sheltered behind their chain-boom, the Greek fleet defied him. If only he could force that boom . . .! He could not even seize its southern anchorage—for that was in Galata, neutral territory belonging to the Republic of Genoa. To enter it would be a *casus belli* which he did not wish to provoke at any price. And while he pondered an idea came to him. . . .

The next day the part of the Turkish camp which surrounded

the Genoese territory of Galata was in an uproar. Labourers moved about with great wooden rollers on their shoulders. An infinite number of navvies were at work, stamping, digging, flattening. Gradually a road came into being out of the uneven earth, running in a strange way from the Bosphorus shore over the heights of Pera to the edge of the Golden Horn, thus uniting two arms of the sea. Along either side of the whole road, the lengths of timber were placed end to end. They were soon to be used as slipways. They were greased with oil, fat and tallow. A *fuste* was hauled out of the Bosphorus; thousands of workmen with teams of oxen, ropes and winches were assembled nearby. Soon everyone was hauling, so that the craft moved along the timber and slowly climbed the hill. It was followed by another *fuste*, and then another. . . . Mahomet's plan was simple: to send part of his Bosphorus fleet into the Channel of the Golden Horn—overland! The attempt was original, but it was also bold, for if the Christians got wind of it not only would the attempt fail, but a large number of ships would be lost. But Mahomet, who was always prudent, had taken many precautions. First of all he chose a size of craft and a number of men which would enable the operation to be completed in 24 hours. Then he arranged several diversions: all day the Turkish bombards had to make a fearful noise cannonading the Byzantine ships, while the remainder of his fleet made another attack on the chain-boom. This combination of boldness and prudence was rewarded. Not for a moment were the Turks disturbed in their work; the Greeks had not the slightest suspicion of what was going on. Here is Barbaro's account of an armada's overland journey:

'The crews which followed each ship, overjoyed by what was going on, and by the thought of what was to come next, boarded their craft, when at the top of the hill, as though they were at sea and quickly travelled downhill towards the Golden Horn. Some of the sailors unfurled the sails and raised shouts of triumph as if they were taking to the high seas, and the wind got into the sails and filled them. Others, sitting on the rowing benches, held their oars in their hands and pretended to row, while the overseers ran up and down the high wooden track spurring on their men with whistles, shouts and lashes from the whip. Thus the Turkish vessels, strange voyagers, slid across the country as if sailing the sea. While the last ones were still ascending the slope of the hill the first were already descending the steep slope to the Golden Horn, all sail set and with great shouts of joy. And it was, I repeat, a strange spectacle to see these vessels with all sail set, with their crews and all their armament, move across the fields as if they were on the high sea.'

*   *   *

It would be impossible to describe the stupor of the Byzantine sentries on the morning of the 23rd when they saw 72 Turkish ships at anchor in the Channel of the Golden Horn. Some thought they had gone mad, others that the Devil was interfering with them. But they had to surrender to the evidence; the enemy was certainly there and the defence plan was overthrown. The situation had suddenly become tragic. Now another side had to be watched: a rampart three miles long, neither high nor strong, through which the Crusaders had captured the city in 1204. And the Greek fleet had lost all the security which the Chain had until then given it.

That day there was in Constantinople a secret conference of the twelve highest ranking military and naval chiefs. The question to be decided was the quickest possible method of destroying the Turkish fleet. The first suggestion was that the whole Byzantine fleet should attack it. This was the best move tactically but diplomatically it was impossible: the Genoese at Galata were terrified of the Sultan and would certainly intervene. 'Let us send soldiers to attack the Turkish camp and set fire to the vessels from the land', suggested others. This would be a most dangerous enterprise, bearing in mind the shortage of fit men in the garrison. Jacomo Coco, a Venetian sailor, had a plan: 'With two galleys I will make a surprise attack on the Turkish fleet and set fire to it.' This proposal was welcomed, put to the vote and adopted.

But there was not a moment to be lost. Everyone pledged himself to secrecy. Coco started to prepare at once and he was ready the next day. He had assembled a flotilla of six vessels: on the one hand, two large swift galleys, and two *fustes*; and on the other two large vessels of about 500 tons, laden with cotton and wool. The idea was that while the latter went on ahead, drawing the fire and acting as a kind of shield, the galleys would slip out unnoticed and rush as quick as lightning upon the Turkish craft. The operation was to start at midnight. Everything was ready by eight o'clock in the evening and no one could hide his impatience. As the hours passed the excitement mounted. The most pious were praying. Others polished their arms. Midnight struck. Everyone moved quickly to his task. And at that very moment a brief order was given: 'Stop! We don't start after all!' What had happened? Everyone ran to the port officer to find out. Two Genoese, it appeared, had arrived from Galata with a message from their *podesta*: 'Delay this expedition for a few days and we shall be able to add our forces to yours.' The offer had been accepted.

Thus, only four days later, on the 28th, did the seven vessels silently move off. It was two hours before dawn. There were two ships loaded with wool and cotton, two Genoese galleys and three *fustes* of twenty-four benches each. Coco had a large amount of inflammable material such as pitch, brushwood and gunpowder and he was confident of victory. From the direction of the Galata Tower there was a flash which for a moment lit up the night. But it was hardly seen before it went out. The Christian crews did not wait to solve the riddle, for they had other things to think about. The darkness and the silence were complete and the vessels slid like phantoms across the water. When they reached Mandrachion Bay, Coco in his impatience decided not to wait for the slower big vessels and threw his galley of 72 oars alone against the Turkish fleet. At this point a frightful noise rent the air and a jet of water flew up—a cannon shot. Consternation amongst the Greeks! The Turks were on the alert! They had been warned! In fact the Genoese of Galata had lost no time in betraying their co-religionists. A second shot whistled over; better aimed, it fell on Coco's galley and went right through it. The galley sank almost at once with the entire crew

Now broke out a deafening cacophony of shouts, drums, trumpets, cymbals, blunderbusses and bombards. The darkness increased with the smoke from the powder; nothing was distinguishable, and the Byzantines sought one another in vain. In the second galley there was a sinister cracking sound; it had been split in the middle by a cannon-ball and was taking in water. The crew tried hurriedly to stop up the holes with their cloaks. But what was the use of carrying on? The fight was lost. The only thing to do was to retreat at full speed, and in the twinkling of an eye the light craft had turned round and fled. But the two large, armoured ships were handicapped by their weight. They tried in vain to break contact. The 72 enemy ships quickly surrounded them. It was an epic battle. For an hour and a half the two bulldogs resisted the yapping mongrels. But their reward came with the dawn when the exhausted Turks turned about, leaving the canal free.

The epilogue was barbaric. The next morning, on the orders of Mahomet, forty Greek sailors who had been captured during the night, were led naked and with hands tied on to the beach in full sight of the garrison. One by one the executioner flung them roughly to their knees and forty times the blade of a scimitar flashed in the sun.

The treachery of the Genoese filled the Byzantines with bitterness and Barbaro exclaimed, 'Oh Genoese dogs. Oh traitors! May God punish you!'

* * *

Misfortunes never come singly! One morning there was a great commotion at the end of the Channel of the Golden Horn where the town walls ended. The Turks were throwing hundreds of barrels into the water. What devilish trick were they preparing now? Anxious, impotent and bewildered the garrison watched hour after hour, day after day, while these barrels were fastened, two abreast, strengthened with wooden beams and covered with planks. A bridge! By this floating road, Mahomet was in process of connecting his two armies, the one that was besieging the land wall with the one near Galata. He would have a wider choice when deciding where to make his next attack. The pontoons were only a few yards from the ramparts—besiegers and besieged were within shouting distance—and big enough to bear pieces of artillery. The garrison, then, might expect to be fired on at point blank range.

What could be done to meet this new threat? Trained troops should be posted to this point of the wall. But where were they to be found? The only thing to be done was to stretch out the defence still further, to demand from everyone an even greater effort. It was decided that henceforth no man should leave the battlements either by day or by night. Food would be bought up by the lame, by women and by children. While this handful of Christians was worn out by ceaseless watch and bombardment, the Musulmans themselves received constant reinforcement and were thus regularly relieved by fresh troops. How could they hold out indefinitely in such conditions?

If only the Venetian fleet would come to the help of the city! The siege had already lasted nearly a month. By an agreement signed on January 26, 1453, the Venetian ambassador had guaranteed that his government would send help when it was needed. The Venetian admiral Loredan had a great reputation—if he appeared in the Bosphorus those cursed infidels would take to their heels! But if he delayed much longer he would find only corpses to liberate. . . . Such were the thoughts of everyone in Byzantium. No one any longer expected salvation except from the West. On May 3 the Basileus called together the leaders of the Venetian community and spoke to them as follows. 'Gentlemen captains, and all of you, nobles of Venice, it becomes evident that your government will not send a fleet to help this unfortunate city. It seems to me that we must send a fast ship to the waters near Negropont to try to find your fleet.' All agreed at once; but would the messenger succeed in getting away? The Turks were everywhere in large numbers. They had even set up a second barrage at the other end of the Bosphorus, at the Dardanelles. It would be a miracle to evade them. But there was no choice. So at midnight a little ship slipped through the boom and out into the silent night. It displayed the Sultan's standard and the crew were dressed in Turkish clothes. It entered the Sea of Marmora and soon reached the Bosphorus, then the Dardanelles. The Turks seemed to take no notice. At last came the open sea, the Mediterranean and the way to the

West and perhaps to salvation. This little vessel bore the hopes of an Empire; it moved as quickly as oars could take it.

Now the garrison beseeched the Basileus to leave too. He could perhaps assemble a relieving army in the Balkans. And if Byzantium fell at least its last Emperor would have been saved. With much dignity he proudly refused. 'I shall never agree to abandon in such misfortune my clergy, the holy churches of the capital, my throne and my people. What would the world say of me? I beg you, on the contrary, to ask me not to leave you. I wish to die here with all of you.'

And the siege continued exhaustingly, day after day. The garrison repelled attack after attack; again and again it rebuilt the walls. But suddenly, during the night of the 16th, an unexpected event occurred. The defenders on the Blachernae side, where the fortifications were weakest because there was no outer wall, heard a dull repetitive noise. At first they paid no attention to it; but it persisted. It seemed to come from under the earth inside the town. Now they listened carefully. . . . Blows, surely! This was important enough to report. John Grant, a clever engineer of German origin, understood at once: the Turks were tunnelling. As they could not get over the ramparts, they were trying to get under them. In order not to attract attention they had started their work far in front of the wall, but now, judging by the sound, they were working a quarter of a mile inside the walls. There was no time to lose and the town was hastily searched for men with mining experience. They were set to work building a counter tunnel and their direction was so good that they had soon burst through into the enemy's. They threw themselves on the bewildered Turks and set fire to their timber work. Soon there was an ominous rumbling: the tunnel had fallen in and the assailants were buried. Again the enemy had been held in check. But any night they could begin again, and could one be warned soon enough each time? Now the garrison had a new anxiety added to its many others, new, insidious, cunning and even more exhausting. The watches became endless when it was not only necessary to search the shadows but to attend to every subterranean sound.

At dawn on May 18 the Turks essayed a new form of attack.

The night had been calm. The sentries at Port St Andrew were satisfied that all was well and strolled about the ramparts awaiting the dawn. But when daylight came the presence of a strange wooden construction, flat against the outside wall, was revealed. It had been manoeuvred into position during less than four hours of darkness and no one had heard a thing! In all haste messengers rushed down the battlements and a few moments later the Emperor and his entire general staff had arrived on the scene. His fears were justified; it was, indeed, a siege tower, and an enormous one. It was so big that it topped the outside wall. A double layer of camel skins protected it from the risk of fire. Projectiles would spend themselves on the earth which filled every chink inside and out. Mounted on numerous wooden rollers it could easily be moved. Steps led to the upper platform where there were assault ladders which could be thrown to the tops of the walls by an ingenious system of ropes. From three frontal openings, as large as windows, archers and arquebusiers could maintain a rain of missiles on the defenders. There were also three lower bays from which sappers could work at undermining the wall or filling in the moat. And as for impeding the work of its occupants—that was indeed a forlorn hope: another thick roof of camel, buffalo and ox hides protected the rollers and steps as well as the quarter-mile path to the camp.

But there was no time to assess the degree of danger; there was time only for urgent counter measures. With frightening shouts the Turks had started to use their tower. Enormous stones were catapulted from the top platform and one of the wall towers crashed down noisily. A breach had been made; moreover, the moat was quickly filling with falling debris. Hundreds of ladders gripped the rock walls and the enemy began to pour in. Now every defender struggled against ten opponents. He had to dodge the projectiles, throw down the loaded ladders, fill in the gaps and counter-attack ceaselessly. The garrison was exhausted, but drew on the energy that despair brings, and night fell before the Turks were able to force a decision. In any case, they intended to complete the task in the morning so they now withdrew, but not without horrible threats. There was no respite for the defenders. In spite of all that had happened, men, women and children worked all through the night and when the sun rose nothing remained of the terrible wounds made in the wall the previous day.

The attacker had to start all over again. Threatening and howling he flung himself into a disorderly attack. But fortune had abandoned him. The battle had hardly started again when immense flames suddenly leaped into the sky—the gigantic siege tower was on fire! With a few lucky shots the defenders had set alight the undergrowth in the ditch and the flames had spread. *'Allah! Allah!'* Gesticulating and lamenting the Turks busied themselves round their engine; but in a few moments the mighty war machine was no more than a heap of cinders. It is said that at the news of the disaster Mahomet ran to the scene and cried in rage: 'If the thirty thousand prophets of Islam had told me that these cursed people would destroy the castle in a single night, I would never have believed them!'

And soon it was the turn of the besiegers to experience misfortune. They erected more siege towers and the garrison destroyed them. They dug more tunnels but each one was located. Burned alive by Greek fire, drowned in floods of water or choked by noxious gases, not one of the sappers escaped.

The conduct of the defenders was beyond all praise. Deprived of sleep, with never any respite, their nerves worn by six weeks of uninterrupted bombardment, they knew all the agonies of a threatened morrow. Death, torture, slavery were more than possibilities. They were fighting one against a hundred and they were badly equipped and half starved. Yet to the very end they forestalled every Turkish trick, to the very end their faith in God did not waver.

By now Mahomet was exhausted. Thirty years previously his father, the Sultan Murad, had been stranded before this town. Rumours persisted that help was imminent. Why not negotiate? So one day he sent an emissary to the Basileus with favourable terms. If Byzantium surrendered, no harm would befall its citizens. They would be free to come and go and they would retain their possessions. Constantine, under Turkish suzerainty, could be King of the Peloponnese. Who would not have been tempted by such terms? But the last Basileus was a hero; he rejected them. 'It is not in my power nor in the power of anyone here to surrender this city. We are ready to die and we shall leave this life without regret.' His action was all the nobler in view of the news he had just received. The little brigantine had returned without having found the Venetian fleet. It had searched the enemy-infested seas of the archipelago; it had sailed north and far to the west, but in vain. Byzantium would receive no help from the West. It was doomed. If the Basileus displayed great courage and integrity, what can one say of the crew of that ship, returning as they did to give an account of their mission? They could easily have saved their own skins, but when their brothers were about to perish for their faith, they thought it their duty to perish with them. Not one sailor failed.

Mahomet himself did not know of the defection of Venice. He would not have believed that the Christian world could be so indifferent. His decision had been made, and he was going to raise the siege. On Sunday the 27th a council of war was held in his tent. Many officers shared the Sultan's views. The Grand Vizir Khalil Pasha—in the pay of Byzantium—was naturally not the last to give his support. His observations and arguments made an impression. How could they hope to vanquish this indomitable garrison? Were not fleets bringing help expected every moment? And even if they took Byzantium, could they hold it? Christianity would never tolerate such a blow to its prestige and, more particularly, to its commerce. Better, then, to go willingly. To give up was not shameful—had not Murad the Great done just that twenty years ago? The majority agreed with the Sultan and the Grand Vizir, and that seemed to settle the matter.

On May 27, 1453, the Moslems were on the point of deciding to withdraw from before Constantinople when Zagan Pasha, the third personage in the Moslem world, sprang to his feet and began to speak. He made everyone ashamed of his slackness, he evoked the riches of Byzantium, the glories of victory. A wild energy emanated from his gestures, and his words were full of fire. The meeting was gradually moved. The young officers trembled with excitement. Mahomet himself was shaken. Finally he decided to consult the army. But as Zagan himself was charged with organizing the referendum, the outcome was not in doubt. In the evening Mahomet was told that the army was strongly in favour of taking the city. And so, after having hovered for a long time, the hand of destiny came down. The Turks were not to raise the siege of Constantinople on May 27, 1453, they were to deliver the final assault!

* * *

The last act of the drama began by night in a frightful uproar. The Turkish camp suddenly became agitated: trumpets and fifes began to be heard and drums rolled, and as if that was not enough, a hundred thousand voices joined in. At the same time lights appeared outside the tents and torches zigzagged amongst them.

The Christian population ran to the ramparts. First of all, hopefully, they thought the enemy was fighting a widespread fire—or perhaps he was preparing to depart. . . . But then they picked out the cries. 'Tomorrow the Christians will be in our hands! We can sell every one of them for a ducat! The priests' beards will make good shoe strings! Their wives and daughters will be our slaves!' Abruptly at midnight it all stopped and all was silent. The sinister vigil of arms had started.

On Monday the 28th the last preparations were hastily completed. Mahomet assembled his officers to issue his final orders. The town was to be attacked on three sides at the same time. The fleet anchored at the Two Columns would attack the West Wall, which edged the Sea of Marmora. The admiral in command would lead his vessels to within firing distance, and while archers, cross-bowmen and fusiliers kept up a continuous barrage, sailors and infantrymen would strive to scale the wall. The Eastern Wall, that which looked on to the Channel of the Golden Horn, would be attacked by troops encamped on the Asian shore and they would have the support of the 72 overland *fustes*. The Northern Wall—the land wall—would be assailed by the main body of the forces at its two weakest points, the Adrianople Gate and the St Romanus Gate. To increase the ardour of his troops, Mahomet made a savage promise: he granted them three days of pillage, three days during which they could do whatever they wanted—kill, torture, violate, rob. 'In Constantinople,' he told them, 'you will find treasure that will make you rich for a hundred years, you will find a multitude of beautiful women, shapely women, ripe young girls still unsullied by men's eyes. You will also find'—this was the East, the Moslem world—'handsome boys. All this is yours.'

There was much activity in Byzantium, too, but it was solemn, funereal. All day the bells had sounded and long processions had moved slowly through the streets chanting the *Kyrie eleison*. Everywhere small groups of priests, bishops, monks, women and children prayed and wept. The holy icons had been paraded and had blessed the most threatened part of the wall. The most solemn and moving moment of that dramatic May 28 came when night had fallen. Everyone knew that the general assault would be made in a few hours. The time could not be spent better than in prayer in Saint Sophia; so the entire people assembled in or near it. This nocturnal office of May 28, 1453, was indeed a solemn occasion; it was the last on which mass was said, the last on which Christ was present in the Great Church. All were present on their knees—Greeks, Genoese and Venetians, Orthodox and Catholic, priests and soldiers, nobles and commons, Basileus and beggars. They were united by a common fervour and made equal by the tragic uncertainty of the city's fate and by the shadow of death. Would the holy mysteries be celebrated there tomorrow? Would these high vaults again witness the communion which now moved so many to tears? The frescoes and mosaics, the lighting, the familiar and sacred things, how precious beyond expression they now seemed!

When everyone had sufficiently conversed with God the men remounted the battlements. A sustained threatening clatter came from the other side of the walls; the mighty Turkish army was ready. To the north and south the vessels were leaving their anchorages and approaching the city. In the west the troops had brought their assault apparatus up to the edge of the foss. The attack could start at any moment.

Constantine moved about on horseback, attended by his faithful servant, blessing his garrison for the last time. He rode along the great length of the wall, pausing from time to time to raise a kneeling man. There can have been few more melancholy scenes in history than this as, ghost-like, the last Basileus moved along the ramparts on the last night of his doomed Empire.

Suddenly, that frightening howling broke out. *'Allah! Allah! La ilahi ila Allah!'* Thousands of trumpets, pipes, cymbals and drums added to the delirium. Innumerable ladders were thrust against the walls. The Sultan's great standard was unfurled. It was between one and two o'clock in the morning and the general assault had begun.

Against the land wall, and especially at the St Romanus Gate, the enemy was going to direct its main effort. Operations against the sea walls were of secondary importance and intended chiefly to immobilize as many defenders as possible, concerning which a few words should first be said.

In the Golden Horn the Moslems launched amphibious attacks. Under a rolling barrage of darts and arrows the infantry advanced across the pontoon bridge, while the famous 72 *fustes* tried to land. But the Christians were every time victorious by showering them with incandescent materials, pitch and oil and Greek fire.

On the Sea of Marmora the Turkish ships from the Two Columns first of all tried to force the chain-boom, but they were repelled by the ten great vessels anchored behind it. The Moslem vessels moved away and the crews disembarked in the badly defended Jewish quarter, which they ravaged from end to end. Once or twice they tried to move further in but each time they were repelled by the garrison, which at that point consisted almost entirely of monks.

At the focal point of the battle, in the Lycus valley, near the St Romanus Gate, John Giustiniani and his seven hundred Genoese were responsible for the defence, and the attack was directed by Mahomet II whose standard dominated the plain. It was between one and two in the morning; it was pitch dark and the garrison awaited the blow. The howling and shouting offered the only point of reference and it grew bigger and bigger. Suddenly a rain of arrows and missiles fell. The enemy had reached the moat and fired. The enemy had reached the foss. Hundreds of ladders were thrust against the wall; frantic monsters climbed them while others held them in position. The tumult, the eternal accompaniment of war, reached its climax. The moment became critical, but the besieged did not panic. They pushed over the loaded ladders, cutting to pieces those who miraculously got to the top and crushing those below with great pieces of rock. The attackers had not expected such resistance; surprised, they began to withdraw. But they were driven to fight by the whip, the scimitar and the iron mace. Roaring and frothing, the wave of assault was flung back against the rampart. Fifty thousand men were driven thus between the Janissaries and Byzantines. The former pierced their backs and the latter slashed their faces. After two hours the force was almost decimated and Mahomet allowed the survivors to leave the field.

Streaming with sweat, their muscles trembling, the garrison laid down their arms, praying for a moment's respite. But almost immediately the tumult broke out again, and a second wave of 50,000 men, fresh and vigorous, broke against the wall. These were not Bashi-bazouks, but the famous Anatolians, tough and scarred, hard in mind and body. An indescribable anguish gripped the defenders. Throughout the town the church bells sounded the alarm and all men who could do so hastened to the battlements. Every second was important. The attackers had already crossed the foss, passed the outer wall and were attacking the emergency stockade. There were rope ladders everywhere and well covered under enormous shields, men were climbing them, climbing tirelessly. The noise continued— the shouts of the fighting men, the rolling of drums, the continuous crackle of muskets and cannon, the cacophony of fifes, cymbals, bells and trumpets. The Byzantines were exhausted, but they turned again to the defence. Again they flung down the ladders and hurled down an avalanche of rock. Again they cut and thrust with axe and sword. But the effort cost them more and more, for they had been fighting ceaselessly for four hours. Then a massive projectile from Urban's cannon knocked a hole in the improvised stockade. Using the screen of smoke and dust a band of Turks at once rushed through the breech.

Now it was hand to hand fighting which reached a rare degree of ferocity. Was this the end? With a final access of energy the garrison succeeded in driving the attackers back, and soon afterwards, sabred, slashed and decimated, the Anatolians in their turn withdrew from the battlefield! The second wave of assault had been broken. Two thousand men, who had experienced two months of incessant watch and tension and starvation, had beaten off more than 100,000 fanatical and experienced Turks after five hours of fighting. Who would not salute such an exploit? Even Critobulus, who had been won over to Mahomet, did not hesitate to write: 'The Romans victoriously repelled the Turks, showing infinite courage and determination. For nothing daunted them, not hunger or complete lack of rest, neither did ceaseless fighting and wounds, nor fear of the massacre with which they were threatened, nor anything however terrible. Nothing weakened their pious zeal, nothing shook them in their courage.'

Mahomet determined to launch a third and final assault. Until then he had held his famous Janissaries in reserve. With the dawn it was possible to follow a more detailed plan of action. With a few brief phrases the Sultan explained his plan and sent his men forward. They ran forward to the attack. But once at the foss archers, cross-bowmen and musketeers stopped, for their firing was to be methodical. It was so organized that it was quite impossible for the defenders to leave their cover. In complete security the Turkish infantry arranged its ladders. The uproar swelled. Drums, tambourines and cymbals sounded the charge, fifes pierced the clamour, cannon and culverins roared. And the whole fantastic cacophony, suggestive of the other world, was punctuated by the piercing leitmotif of *'Allah! Allah!'* On the Greek side the din was no less. The bells ceaselessly rang, their hammers calling lugubriously for help. A thousand voices shouted 'To the walls!' 'Help!' Confusion reigned everywhere. All along the foot of the wall the Janissaries were falling over one another in their haste to scale the walls. Up there, behind the battlements women, children and old men ran desperately to and fro in a cloud of smoke and dust, amongst the falling arrows, carrying munitions to the combatants. *'Allah! Allah! Allah! Allah!'* The shouts came nearer and nearer; then the heads of the leading Janissaries, wild and ferocious, appeared above the top of the stones. Not all the ladders were pushed over, and the enemy took foothold and leapt inside.

There was furious hand to hand fighting in the *peribolous*. Giustiniani and his little troop of heroes thrust and parried and hacked. Where did they get the strength and courage to fight like that after so many hours of terrible effort? Fighting a hundred to one they contained the furious thrust; they even gained a little ground. Was the enemy going to be thrown back for a third time? Already his effort was weakening. Transported with joy the Emperor Constantine had a momentary glimpse of victory. . . . But alas! A tragic incident suddenly developed. In the distance, above the towers on the ramparts, in the direction of the Adrianople Gate, the garrison saw Mahomet's standards flying. So the Turks had succeeded in forcing the defences at that point! They must be already in Byzantium and one was threatened from behind! What had happened? In that part of the inner wall, half below ground level, there was a little gate which opened directly into the city. It was called the *kerkoporta*, or Circus Gate, and it was so obscured that only the older men remembered its existence. At a certain moment it had been opened for the purpose of hasty revictualling and—a fatal oversight—it had not been closed again. This might not have mattered—as most citizens had failed to notice it in recent years it might have escaped the eyes of the Turks. But misfortune willed it otherwise, first by reason of the fact that the outer wall had collapsed, and next that a group of Janissaries had come across it. Automatically they tried the lock which, to their great surprise, responded to pressure, and they found themselves inside the city. In a few moments a veritable human torrent was flowing into Byzantium. Surprised from the rear, the garrison of the inner wall was cut to pieces and soon the Sultan's banner was floating from the nearby towers. This incident in itself might not have been of any great consequence if it had remained unknown, for quickly enough Greek reinforcements appeared which succeeded in repelling and even ejecting the attackers. But the banner was seen, and the conclusions drawn . . . wrongly! The men at the St Romanus Gate were persuaded that they would soon be attacked from the rear. They were thoroughly alarmed, drew back, and began to be demoralized.

Would they eventually get a grip on themselves? Such a valiant group might well have done so, but at that moment the worst conceivable thing happened. John Giustiniani fell, struck by a pike. Not one of the chroniclers differs in his assessment of the consequences of this event. The entire defence was staggered by it. It was in vain that the Basileus tried to sustain his men. This is the kind of incident which determines the issue of a battle and the very face of history. Mahomet uttered a cry of triumph. Victory at last was in his grasp! He leapt forward from the moat and shouted to his Janissaries. 'The city is ours! It is ours already! See, there is no one left to defend it! Fear not! Follow me! The city is ours!' The reply was a frenzied howling, and a furious wave struck the wall. It flowed over the emergency wall and the debris of the ramparts.

Now the Byzantines fled in disorder. Some were flung into the moat and killed, others were chased and cut down from behind. There was nothing to stop the incoming tide. The last gates were swept down and a turbulent wave, cascading and roaring, spilled over the city. Yes, this was the end. On this May 29, 1453, fell the empire which had endured for more than a thousand years. And on this day Christianity disappeared from the Eastern sky. What can the thoughts of the last Basileus have been? Why should he live? He dismounted and slowly divested himself of the Imperial insignia, retaining of it only the red campagia—those famous boots ornamented with two-headed eagles—and plunged into the hand to hand fighting. He thrust to right and to left, and then suddenly vanished. Much later they found his body and Mahomet caused it to be decapitated. Then for many months to come, accompanied by forty captive young men and forty captive virgins, it was displayed throughout Asia to announce the triumph of the Crescent to the remotest corners.

* * *

And this is how this precious city was destroyed. . . .

The first picture which history offers us of this Dantesque hell is one of breathtaking violence. This was the feast day of St Theodosia. Slowly a procession of women, children and old men moved out of the rose-covered church dedicated to her. Everyone was wearing his or her best clothes and white-bearded priests held on high the comforting images of Christ and his gentle Mother, the Theotokos. Suddenly there burst on the scene a disordered mass of shouting monsters, their faces streaked with sweat, half-naked and blood-bespattered. What followed may be imagined. The procession broke up, but they were caught almost immediately and a few minutes later thousands of hacked and disembowelled and decapitated bodies reddened the slabs and the gutters.

Such scenes were to be seen everywhere. Drunk with slaughter, the Turks massacred throughout the morning. Nothing, and certainly not pity, stayed their hands. Like madmen the unhappy Christians ran about the streets, shouting, weeping, pleading, until lance, scimitar or knife stretched them on the pavement in their blood. Inside the houses women were dragged by the hair to windows and pushed through, old men were cut down, children were stabbed with pikes under the very beds where they hid.

When the orgy of killing had spent itself, rape took its place. Here is an extract from Critobulus, the Christian renegade who had entered the Sultan's service.

'Nothing will ever equal the horror of this harrowing and terrible spectacle. People frightened by the shouting ran out of their houses and were cut down by the sword before they knew what was happening. And some were massacred in their houses where they tried to hide, and some in churches where they sought refuge. The enraged Turkish soldiers . . . gave no quarter. When they had massacred and there was no longer any resistance they were intent on pillage and roamed through the town stealing, disrobing, pillaging, killing, raping, taking captive men, women, children, old men, young men, monks, priests, people of all sorts and conditions . . . there were virgins who awoke from troubled sleep to find those brigands standing over them with bloody hands and faces full of abject fury. This medley of all nations, these frantic brutes stormed into their houses, seized them, dragged them, tore them, forced them, dishonoured them, raped them at the crossroads and made them submit to the most terrible outrages. It is even said that at the mere sight of those savages many girls were so stupefied that they almost gave up the ghost. Old men of venerable appearance were dragged by their white hair and piteously beaten, and beautiful children of noble family were carried off. Priests were led into captivity in batches as well as reverend virgins, hermits and recluses who were dedicated to God alone and lived only for

Him to whom they sacrificed themselves, who were dragged from their cells and others from the churches in which they had sought refuge, in spite of their weeping and sobs and their emaciated cheeks, to be made objects of scorn before being struck down. Tender children were brutally snatched from their mothers' breasts and girls were pitilessly given up to strange and horrible unions and a thousand other terrible things happened.'

With senses satisfied the Turks gave themselves up to pillage. Shops, houses, palaces, churches—nothing was spared. Let us turn again to Critobulus.

'Temples were desecrated, ransacked and pillaged . . . sacred objects were scornfully flung aside, the holy icons and the holy vessels were desecrated. Ornaments were burned, broken in pieces or simply thrown into the streets. Saints' shrines were brutally violated in order to get out the remains which were then thrown to the wind. Chalices and cups for the celebration of the mass were set aside for their orgies or broken or melted down or sold. Priests' garments embroidered with gold and set with pearls and gems were sold to the highest bidder and thrown into the fire to extract the gold. Immense numbers of sacred and profane books were flung on to the fire or torn up and trampled underfoot. However, the majority were sold at derisory prices, for a few pence. Saints' altars, torn from their foundations were overturned. All the most holy hiding places were violated and broken in order to get out the holy treasures which they contained.'

Amongst all these outrages the profanation of Saint Sophia stood out. In the great church an immense crowd was assembled, praying despairingly. The famous bronze doors had been closed, and full of anguish all awaited the imminent arrival of the conquerors. Suddenly violent blows shook and broke down the doors, and a tide of blood-covered brutes swept into the holy place. To make room for themselves they began by using the pike and scimitar a little; but they were in the grip of covetousness, not sadism. Here, they said to themselves as they looked about, fortune awaits us. In an instant, all who were young, good-looking and healthy were stripped, despoiled and herded. High-born women, young and gentle girls of noble family, now naked under their long hair, fell thus into slavery. Their masters bound them with whatever was at hand: sashes, belts, kerchiefs, stoles, tent ropes, camel and horse reins. With blows and kicks they were herded outside into long columns, to be led to a shameful fate and to all the extremities of the Islamic world.

Then came the turn of the Church where generations of the pious had added to the store of sacred treasures. There were vases of gold and silver studded with pearls and precious stones, sacerdotal garments of prodigious richness, reliquaries, icons and luminaries. All were broken open, pillaged and destroyed. To amuse their comrades some capered about in priests' robes, holding up a crucifix surmounted by a turban. The famous relics which had protected the town—the bodies of the most illustrious martyrs, the most glorious champions of orthodoxy, and the most celebrated icons—were wrenched from their settings of precious metal and thrown out amongst the dead bodies and wandering dogs. In all history only the sack of Jerusalem can compare with this! To make their attitude quite clear the Turks stabled their camels there and installed their public women; and the Church of the Holy Wisdom became a stable and a brothel.

The orthodox still recount a legend which has come down to them from this tragic time. At the very moment that the great church was attacked the wall behind the altar opened and the priest who was officiating disappeared into it, bearing the holy chalice, and the wall closed up again. When at last an orthodox ruler returns to Constantinople, that priest will emerge from the wall and complete the mass which was so tragically interrupted many centuries ago.

As for the Sultan, he was sensual rather than acquisitive, and more interested in people than in goods. Phrantzes, the faithful servant of the Basileus, has recounted the fate of his young and good-looking family. His three daughters were consigned to the Imperial harem, even the youngest, a girl of fourteen who died there in despair. His only son, John, a fifteen-year-old boy, was killed by the Sultan himself for having repelled his advances. The Basileus was survived by his brother, the Grand Duke

Lukas Notaras, the second personage of the Empire and a man of great intelligence and ability. At first the Sultan covered him with honours and discussed with him the possibility of his becoming governor of the town, with responsibility for clearing up and repopulation. One night, having been told of the graces of Notaras' youngest son, he sent a eunuch to fetch him. When Notaras told the Sultan that his religion did not permit him to consent to so ignominious a proposal, the Sultan was seized with anger and caused both the boy and his brother and father to be brought before him. Then he summoned the executioner. Notaras asked to be put to death last in order, says Critobulus, 'that his children perhaps fearing death, might not be tempted to renounce their faith to purchase their lives'. Standing there pale-faced, but without lowering his eyes, Notaras saw his two sons decapitated. He prayed and in his turn bowed his head to the blade. As for the Sultan, it pleased him to stare for some time at the faces of his three victims.

Critobulus has assessed the impact on Byzantium of the events of those few days in spring 1453.

'Constantinople seemed to have been visited by a hurricane or to have been burnt in some fire. It became suddenly silent. . . . The Turkish sailors were extremely active in bringing about this destruction for they upset, undermined and turned upside down everything more thoroughly than the Persian Datis at Eritrea. They broke temples, chapels, ancient shrines, tombs, crypts, vaults and all the most secret hiding places. They examined everything. They pulled everybody and everything out of their hiding places. . . . The whole army, both of land and sea, flooded through the town from break of day till nightfall, pillaging and wrecking and carrying booty back to camp and ship. Nevertheless there were some like hawks who took hold of things, crept away stealthily and returned straight home. In this manner was the whole city emptied and depopulated and destroyed as though by a fire and changed into a tomb. Seeing it thus one would have found it hard to believe that it ever contained men's homes, wealth, abundance or any goods or ornaments, and that in a city which had been so brilliant and great. Now there were only deserted dwellings, which by their tomb-like appearance instilled terror in the minds of those who contemplated them.

The same author tells an interesting story about the Sultan. 'When he saw the ravages, the destruction and the deserted houses and all that had perished and become ruins, then a great sadness took possession of him and he repented the pillage and all the destruction. Tears came to his eyes and sobbing he expressed his sadness. "What a town this was! And we have allowed it to be destroyed!" His soul was full of sorrow. And in truth it was natural, so much did the horror of the situation exceed all limits.'

It was, we said at the beginning of this chapter, over a simple question of winds that Byzantium fell. The Christian fleet bearing reinforcements had been off Chios for a month, waiting for a wind. The little brigantine had passed nearby without seeing it. During a whole month it would have sufficed if the weather had been favourable for just one day; then would the Turks have raised the siege and hastily withdrawn. One windy day— on such things hang the fate of empires and the course of history.

INDEX

A

Abasgians, 7, 107
Abramite monastery, 129, 149
Abydos, 103
Academy of Sciences, 51
Acropolis, 198
Adalbert, 175
Administration, 81, 107, 110–11
Adrianople, 188, 9, 194
Aegaion Pelagos, 109
Agriculture, 67
Aigues-Mortes, 190
Aix-la-Chapelle, 102
Albigensian heresy, 51
Aleppo, 122, 4
Alexander, 72–3
Alexius Comnenus, 27, 30, 4, 58
Alhallabah Palace, 124
Alypios, Saint, 66
Amalfi, 165, 179
Amastrianon Forum, 25
Amazons, 48
Anarzabe, 126
Anastasius, 70
Anatolia, -ians, 111, 5, 8, 214
Ancona, 181, 3
Andrew, Saint, 181
Andronicus, 39, 57
Anemas, 44
Anthimus, Patriarch, 38
Anthusa, 52
Apambas, *see* Argyros, Marianos
Apulia, 163, 175
Arapastos, 130
Archangel Michael, 116
Aregeus, Mount, 117
Ariadne, 35
Arithmetic, 66
Armenia, -ians, 107–8, 117, 127, 140–1, 144
Army, 32, 41–5, 50–1, 107–27
Arsinos, 66
Art, 46, 58
Artemidorus, 115
Artemius, Saint, 64
Asclepiodorus, 59
Assyrians, 176

Astronomy, 66–7
Athanasius, 59
Attila, 130
Autocrator, *see* Basileus
Auxerre, 102
Avars, 165
Avignon, 190

B

Balkans, 118, 189, 207
Baltagou, 188, 9, 200, 1
Banking, 98, 103
Barbaro, quoted, 188–9, 191–2, 194–6, 199, 202–3, 205
Barcetta, 165
Bardas Phocas, 144–6, 175
Bardinius, 71
Bari, 166, 171
Bashi-bazouks, 188, 214
Basil I, 7, 25, 7, 31, 71–2, 104, 140
Basil II, 23
Basil, Bishop, 29
Basil, Saint, 166
Basil the Bastard, 144, 6, 7, 172
Basileus: apartments, 23–4; on campaign, 112–17; impersonates Christ, 17–22, 149, 150–1; clothing, 17–18, 114, 129, 142, 9, 151, 170; coronation, 107; and Factions, 57; at the games, 57, 61; and gold, 45; power, 26–8; receptions, 19; social origins, 31, 47; victory parades, 41–5
Basilic (cannon), 194
Basilissa, 24, 32–7
Bederiana, 31
Benedict, Saint, 166
Bessarion, 8
Bythinia, -ians, 118, 149
Black Sea, 99, 103, 117
Bocciardi brothers, 190
Bogomile doctrine, 50–1
Book of Ceremonies, 62
Bosphorus, 112, 9, 144, 8–9, 188–9, 194, 202, 6
Boucoleon, 112
Bouïd, Sultan, 128

Bringas, 135–46
Brya, 176
Bucellarian theme, 111
Bucoleon Palace, 155
Bulgaria, Bulgars, 7, 73–4, 99, 107–8, 110, 154, 165, 173
Bury, quoted, 104
Byzantium, the capital, 27, 40, 5, 68, 86–8, 104, 112, 130–2, 149, 161, 178, 183

C

Caesar Bardas, 72
Caesarea, 111, 7, 141
Calabria, 163, 6, 175
Cappadocia, 117
Carcassonne, 190
Caria, 24
Cassiodorus, 162
Cantanzaro, 165
Catazaron, 165
Caucasus, 7
Cedrenus, quoted, 136–8
Ceylon, 7, 103
Chain-boom, 190, 4, 6, 200–3, 213
Chalcedon, 112
Chariot racing, 54–7, 60–4
Charlemagne, 102
Charon, 34
Charsian, 111
Charsios, 111
China, 7, 99, 100, 103
Chios, 222
Christopher, Emperor, 172, 3
Christophoros, 178
Chronicus, quoted, 55
Chrysopolis, 112, 144, 7
Cibyraioton, 109
Cilicia, -ians, 112, 126–7, 136
Circus, see Hippodrome
Coco, Jacomo, 203–4
Constans, 26
Constantine I, the Great, 19, 26, 68, 129, 153, 178
Constantine V, Copronymus, 28, 32, 52, 8
Constantine VII, Porphyrogenitus, 7, 25, 62, 101, 9, 137–9, 144
Constantine IX, Monomachus, 7
Constantine Dragases, 7, 207, 9, 210, 2, 6, 7

Constantine Margarites, 107
Constantinople, see Byzantium
Contarini, 190
Convent of World Redemption, 30
Corfu, 181
Corner, 190
Courcouas family, 140
Couvade, 34
Craftsmanship, 101
Creed, the, 147–8
Crete, 139
Crimea, 7
Critobulus, quoted, 189, 199, 215, 218–9, 221–2
Croatians, 7, 108
Crusaders, Crusades, 7, 183, 9, 203
Currency, 102–3

D

Dalassenas, 34
Damascus, 66
Daniel, 66
Danube, Danube valley, 32, 109
Dardanelles, 206
Datis, 221
Delphi, 59
Denzerichos, 130
Diedo, Aloisio, 190–2
Diehl, quoted, 36, 8, 69, 108
Digenes Akritas, 34
Diomedes, 71
Dionisiades of Eleusis, 63
Dolfin, 190
Dolma Bagcha Palace, 194
Dorylaeum, 115, 6
Dress, 60, 8, 116, 161, 177, 8
Dukas, 25
Dyrrachion, 111

E

Ecclesiasticus, 152
Economic policy, 88–104
Eddauleh, Shiekh, 124, 7
Emperor, see Basileus
Empress, see Basilissa
Epiphanius of Cyprus, 51
Equalitarianism, 29
Eritrea, 221
Eski-Shehir, 115
Ethiopia, -ians, 7, 108

INDEX

Eudocia, 23, 6
Eunuchs, 46–8
Euphrates, 58, 108, 112, 8
Euphrozyme, 33
Evodision, 179

F

Factions, 22, 7, 37, 42–3, 53–7, 61–4, 130–2, 149–52, 167
Febronia, Saint, 64
Ferradou, quoted, 85
Figi Palace, 174
Florence, 8
Florence, Council of, 193
Food, 22, 63, 114, 173
France, 107
Frederick Barbarossa, 107
Frontiers, 108

G

Galahad, quoted, 47, 55
Galata, 190, 7, 200–4
Gallipoli, 189
Gelzer, quoted, 109
Gemistus Plethon, 8
Gennadios, 8
Genoa, -ese, 190, 2, 7, 201–5, 212–13
Geoponics, 67
George Scholarios, 193
Germans, Germany, 99, 107, 161, 173, 6
Giustiniani, John, 190, 6, 213–16
Glegoris, 166
Godfrey de Bouillon, 115
Golden Gate, 42, 129, 149, 165, 7
Golden Horn, 30, 147, 187, 190–1, 197–205, 211, 3
Goths, 7, 50, 107
Gourgen family, 140
Grant, John, 207
Greece, Ancient, 8, 58, 69, 70
Greek fire, 109, 119, 123, 200, 9, 213
Greek language, 117, 161, 3, 5
Greek Orthodox Church, 52, 162, 193
Gregory, Bishop of Nyssa, 49
Gregory II, Pope, 163, 6
Guilds, 95, 7

H

Hagar, 128
Hagia Sophia, *see* St Sophia
Hamdanide, 112, 139
Harold, 109
Hebdomon, port, 128
Hebdomon Palace, 191
Heraclius, 7, 25, 50, 64, 110, 130
Hiereia Palace, 20
Himyar, 107
Hippodrome, 25, 9, 31, 9, 42–5, 52–3, 59, 61–4, 70, 131
Hippodromes, 55
Hodna, 108
Holidays, 94
Holy Apostles, Church, 37, 44, 52
Holy Roman Empire, 161, 7
Homer, 51, 67, 9
Hospitals, etc., 29–30
Hungarians, 7
Huns, 7, 73

I

Iberians, 118
Icasia, 34
Icons, iconoclasts, iconodules, 17–18, 45, 51–3, 150, 163–4, 212, 9, 220
Igor, Prince, 119
India, 99
Ionian Sea, 118
Irene, 32, 68–9
Italy, 8, 100, 118, 161–3, 169

J

Janissaries, 188, 198, 214–17
Japan, 100
Jerusalem, 220
Jews, 39–41, 90, 213
John Chrysostom, Saint, 22
John Italus, 107
John the Damascene, 69
John the Orphanotrophos, 29
John Palaeologios, 191
John, Patriarch, 63
John XIII, Pope, 177, 180
Justin I, 31
Justinian, 7, 28, 31, 8, 50, 5, 8, 108, 152, 162

K

Khalil Pasha, Grand Vizir, 192, 210
Khazars, 7, 118
Kosmas, 103
Kouroupas of Crete, 44
Kroum, King of Bulgaria, 109
Kynegion, 191

L

La Brocquière, 69
Landolf of Beneventum, 176, 180
Landowners, 81–6
Lebanon, 118
Lebeau, quoted, 47
Lecapenus, 29
Legal system, 17
Lenormant, quoted, 8, 166
Leo I, 31
Leo III the Isaurian, 31–2, 51, 71, 164–5
Leo IV the Khazar, 32
Leo V, 31, 71
Leo VI, 25–7
Leo the Deacon, quoted, 140
Leo Phocas, 147, 168–9, 172, 6, 9, 180
Leucadia, 181
Literature, 69
Liudprand, Bishop of Cremona, 162, 166–83
Liudprand, Lombard King, 163
Longobardia, -bards, 171, 6
Loredan, Admiral, 206
Lupicina, Basilissa, 32
Lycandox, 111
Lycaonia, 117
Lycus valley, 195, 213

M

Macedonia, -ians, 117–18, 144, 6
Magnaura Palace, 20, 36, 149
Mahomet II, 60, 183, 8–9, 196–7, 200–6, 209–22
Malabar coast, 7
Malagina, 115
Maleinos, Saint, 154
Mandrachion Bay, 204
Marcianus, 72
Marcus Aurelius, 111
Mardaites, 118
Marianos Argyros, 140, 4, 6
Marie-Irene, 172

Marmora, Sea of, 187–8, 190, 206, 211, 3
Massissa, 127
Matriarchal tendency, 34
Maximus the Pagan, 129
Medical theories, 64, 7
Mercenary soldiers, 118–19
Mese, the, 130, 150, 167
Mesopotamia, 111
Messina, 165
Methymna, 139
Michael II, 71, 107
Michael III, 7, 25, 31, 58
Michael Lachanodracon, 52
Michael the Stammerer, 33, 71
Michael Stratioticus, 26–7
Michael Rangabé, 71
Miletus, 165
Military strategy, tactics, 119–27
Mirobolion, 69
Mocenigo, 190
Moesia, 7
Monasteries, monks, 85, 107
Monastery of the Pantocrator, 193
Monuments, 59
Moravians, 7, 108
Moschos, John, 103
Most Holy Theotokos, Church, 150
Murad II, Sultan, 209–10
Murad IV, Sultan, 60
Mycenae, 59
Mytilene, 139

N

Naples, 47
Narentians, 7
Naupactos, 180
Negropont, 206
New Palace, 23
Nicephorus the Logothete, 110
Nicephorus II, Phocas, 5, 122–3, 135–57, 168–80
Nicodemia, Gulf of, 111, 3
Nicopolis, 111
Normans, 107, 118, 163
Notaras, Grand Duke, 196, 221

O

Opsikon, 111, 4
Optimate, 111

INDEX

Orban, 194, 214
Origen, 69
Orontes, 112
Otranto, 163, 180, 1
Otto I, 162
Otto II, 166, 171-2, 175-80
Otto III, 102

P

Palermo, 165
Pandolf of Capua, 176, 180
Paphlagonia, 32
Parthenius, Bishop, 72
Paschal, 144
Patrae, 72
Patras, Gulf of, 181
Patriarch, 20, 6, 42, 3, 7, 52, 60, 131, 147, 151-3, 193, 6
Pausanius, 59
Pearl Triclinium, 33
Peasantry, 81-6
Pege Monastery, 20
Peloponnese, 118, 189, 209
Pera, 192, 4, 202
Persia, -ians, 73, 99, 100, 165
Petchenegs, 7
Peter, Bulgarian King, 172-3
Phargans, 118
Philaretus, 29
Philarios, 29
Philocale, 94
Philotus, Bishop of Euchaitia, 143-4
Philosophy, 69
Philoxenus, 68
Phocas, 25, 31, 63-4, 130
Phocas family, 29
Photius, 69
Phrantzes, quoted, 200, 220
Plataea, battle, 59
Polyeuctes, Patriarch, 137-9, 145-6, 148, 152, 174
Pope, 162-3, 174, 8, 180, 192
Porphyrogenitus, the title, 24
Prisoners of war, 21, 39, 41-5, 129, 220
Procopius of Caesarea, 100, 9
Propontis, 154
Psellos, 29
Ptolemy, 66
Public health, 64, 8
Punishments, 25-6, 38-9, 57-8, 96-7

R

Rambaud, quoted, 25, 54, 8, 63, 9, 70
Ravenna, 163
Refugees, religious, 52
Religious controversy, 48-53
Renaissance, 8
Romanus I, Lecapenus, 25, 7, 31, 101, 139, 144, 172
Romanus II, 135, 9, 144
Romanus IV, 40
Romanus Courcouas, 141
Rome, 163, 173, 190
Rome, Ancient, 41, 63, 8, 9, 161, 171
Roumeli Hissar, fortress, 188, 9
Runciman, quoted, 102
Russia, -ians, 7, 73, 90, 9, 107, 117-18, 145

S

Sacred Palace, 19, 22-4, 36, 57, 72, 88, 99, 112, 131, 2, 6, 141, 6, 168, 173, 6, 8
St John the Baptist, Church, 64
St John the Evangelist, Church, 129
St John Hebdomon, Church, 149
St Mary, Blachernae, 52, 65
St Stephens, Chapel, 57
Salerno, 165
Samos, 109
St Sophia, 19, 37, 42, 3, 52, 61, 70, 88, 108, 131, 7, 145, 6, 151, 169, 187, 193, 6, 212, 219-20
Sangarius, 115
Saracens, 44, 73, 96, 111, 2, 6, 9, 120, 3, 145, 150, 165, 177
Saxon Council, 174
Scandinavia, 110, 8, 145
Science, 66
Scutari, 144
Scythia, -ians, 144
Seleucia, 111
Seljuks, 115
Senate, Senators, 26-7, 32, 5, 138-9, 143-4, 147, 151, 2, 3
Serbs, 7, 108
Sex equality, 34, 66
Sicily, 107
Sieburg Cathedral, 102
Siege warfare, 121-7
Silk, 7, 90-3, 9, 100
Simeon, Bulgarian Tsar, 27, 73
Sisinnos, 172

Slavery, slaves, 96, 126
Slavesians, 118
Slavs, 7, 118
Sparta, 59
Spiridion, Saint, 193
Stephen, Emperor, 139
Strymon, 118
Stylites, 66
Suleiman the Magnificent, 60
Symeon, 172
Syria, 89, 93, 8, 100

Tornice family, 144
Toulmates, 118
Trade, 90, 98–103
Trevisan, 190–1
Tribune Palace, 57
Triclinium Hall, 36, 169
Tunisia, 108
Turks, 47, 118, 188–222
Two Columns, 194, 7, 8, 211, 3
Tzamandos, 136, 9, 140–1
Tzimisces, John, 140–3, 154–7, 172

T

Tana, 191
Tarentum 165
Tarsus, 55
Tatta, Lake, 117
Taurus, 119
Taurus Mountains, 112, 127
Taxation, 103–4, 109–11
Tembri, 114
Temple of the Most Holy Theotokos, 129
Theodora, 27, 32, 8, 72
Theodosia, Saint, 217
Theodosius I, 70
Theodosius II, 66, 129, 191
Theodosius, port, 149
Theophano, 135–6, 154–6
Theophilus, Emperor, 26, 31, 7–8, 52, 60, 128
Theophylact the Insufferable, 29
Theophylact, Patriarch, 138
Theotokos, *see* Virgin Mary
Thessalonica, 111, 8
Thessaly, 24, 118
Thibaut, Duke of Spoleto, 47–8
Thomas the Usurper, 71
Thrace, -ians, 115, 7, 149
Thrymbos, 115

U

Urban, 194, 214

V

Vallenza, 165
Vardar, river, 118
Vatican, 173
Venice, Venetians, 107, 179, 188–9, 191–2, 206, 210, 2
Verangians, 145, 153
Virgil, quoted, 83
Virgin of Hodigitria, 165–6
Virgin Mary, 18, 50, 65, 103
Vitellius, 63
Vladimir, Russian prince, 108

X

Xerxes, 59

Z

Zagan Pasha, 210
Zealots, 193
Zeno, Emperor, 35, 68
Zeuxippos baths, 44, 131
Zoë, Empress 27, 9